Your Hidden Half

Your Hidden Half

Blending
Your Private
and Public Self

A Quest for
Personal Wholeness

Mark R. McMinn

BAKER BOOK HOUSE
Grand Rapids, Michigan 49516

Copyright 1988 by
Baker Book House Company

Printed in the United States of America

Scripture quotations used are from the New American Standard Bible,
copyright 1960, 1962, 1963, 1968, 1971, 1972, 1973, 1975, 1977 by The
Lockman Foundation.

Persons identified as "clients" in this book represent a composite of
Dr. McMinn's practice, and no one individual is portrayed in this book.

Library of Congress Cataloging-in-Publication Data

McMinn, Mark R.
    Your hidden half.

        1. Identification (Religion)   I. Title.
BV4509.5.M36   1988   233   88-22267
ISBN 0-8010-6243-8

To
Lisa
my wife, colleague, best friend,
and the most authentic person I know

Contents

Preface

As a child, I loved to look under the rocks in the tidal pools of the Oregon coast. I would cautiously place my hands near the bottom of the rock and then quickly jerk it upward, causing the rock to flip over and the wildlife underneath to run for shelter. Miniature crabs would run every direction as they sensed danger. Then I would walk a few more feet, find another rock, and repeat the process. There were dozens of crabs underneath some of the rocks, only a few crabs under others.

Now I look under rocks for a living. As a Christian psychologist, I commonly see the wildlife underneath the hard exterior of personality. On the outside, the rocks look strong. They are marbled with Christian dedication, Christ-like desires, and altruistic behavior. But underneath the rocks I often find another world—a world of animal-like impulse and chaos.

Looking strong on the outside is one thing Christians do well. And having wildlife underneath our exteriors is also very common. Unfortunately, we sometimes can't handle it. Our critics notice our duality. Imagine the following survey.

Ask one hundred people what they think of when they hear the term *Christianity*. Those sympathetic to Christianity, perhaps a minority of the one hundred, will give positive responses: "A Christian has faith in Christ," "Christians have a personal relationship with Jesus Christ," "Christianity is a common religion in Western societies," and so on. But what will the others say?

My guess is that some will pick up on the theme of duality. "Christians play church on Sundays in order to relieve guilt about the rest of their week." "I don't care about Christians because they are all a bunch of hypocrites." "All I know about Christianity is that Jim and Tammy Bakker are frauds!" Our critics see Christians as two-faced, living one life in public and another in private. They see duality more than sincerity. They see under our rocks rather than being impressed with the rock itself.

This book looks at the reasons for duality. Christians don't mean to be two-faced. We often have great motivation to change, but can't seem to find effective ways to change. So we keep our dual nature hidden. We all have secrets we wouldn't bring up in a prayer meeting or a Sunday-evening church service. We have regrets about mistakes from the past and yet we seek a higher calling. We strive to let God control our lives but we often fall short. So we talk one life and live another.

The answer is not to go around flipping over one another's rocks, exposing all the secrets of life. Neither is the answer to hide all the evil in our personalities, stuffing more and more under the rock. But somewhere in between these two extremes there is hope for personal wholeness. By being aware of what is under our own rocks and being vulnerable enough to show one or two others, we can learn to grow and deal with duality.

MARK R. MCMINN
Newberg, Oregon

Acknowledgments

Being credited as the sole author of this book doesn't seem quite right. Although I sat in front of my computer typing all the words, many of the ideas were distilled from numerous conversations and interactions with those I know.

My faculty colleagues at George Fox College are a constant source of intellectual stimulation. They encourage me to think openly and critically, but also Christianly. Dr. Jim Foster, division chair and fellow psychologist, has been a role model and an encourager. Dr. Lee Nash, vice president for academic affairs, has protected my writing time from trivial institutional assignments and supported my scholarship in the midst of a busy teaching schedule. Lee also has stimulated my thinking with his insightful critiques of Christian extremism.

Throughout my training I have been fortunate to work with leaders in the scientific study of psychology. Dr. Martin Katahn and Dr. Kenneth Wallston at Vanderbilt University taught me how to think scientifically and encouraged my academic growth. Dr. Arthur Wiens at the Oregon Health Sciences University helped me see clinical practice as a scientific endeavor throughout my internship and residency.

My clinical colleagues at Northwest Psychological Associates and Beaverton Family Counseling Center have been helpful in my professional development. Dr. Gordon McMinn, my father and counseling colleague, has spent many hours with me discussing ways of conceptualizing counseling and emotional problems. His input is more important than he knows.

Publishing a first book is always difficult and I have especially appreciated the editorial staff at Baker Book House. They have encouraged, educated, and supported me.

My biggest debt is to Lisa, my wife and mother of our three daughters, Danielle, Sarah, and Megan. Lisa is the gifted writer in our family and she spent scores of hours reading my words, suggesting changes, reading the revisions, and so forth. Her patience, like her editing, is incredible!

1

Duality

> ...when I reached years of reflection, and began
> to look round me and take stock of my progress
> and position in the world, I stood already
> committed to a profound duplicity of life....
>
> Dr. Jekyll

With agony Dr. Henry Jekyll wrote these final words. He was losing control. The duplicity characterizing his existence ran wild. Mr. Hyde's hidden face once took a strong potion to produce, but now appeared without warning. The evil Mr. Hyde took over as the benevolent Dr. Jekyll slipped slowly into oblivion. Suicide was Jekyll's escape from the duality painted so vividly in the fictional work of Robert Louis Stevenson.

Such striking contrast is rarely the case, but duplicity in human nature is widespread. We constantly battle our evil with our desire for rightness. The battle rages on, sometimes producing hopelessness, stagnation, and powerlessness. It is symptomatic of the human condition. Duality haunts us at every age: riddling us as children, devastating us as adolescents, confusing us as adults, drawing its power from a seemingly endless reservoir.

Perhaps as a psychologist, I see the duality of others more than most. Pastor *A*'s church releases him because of his extramarital affair with an active church member. Mr. *B* frequently screams profanity at his children when they act irresponsibly. Mrs. *C* loses control and strikes her children in anger. Ms. *D* would be horrified if anyone in the church found out about her alcohol-abuse problem. Examples of duality go on and on. It affects us all—television evangelists, politicians, business executives, church leaders, homemakers, doctors, students, salespersons, and educators. No one is exempt from the subtle pathology of the Jekyll/Hyde syndrome.

Evangelical Christians have done a good job identifying and modeling the upright Dr. Jekyll personality. Unfortunately, we have done a poor job coping with Mr. Hyde. We discuss taking off the old self and putting on the new. We develop new methods of Bible study, discipling, and prayer. In the process we unintentionally communicate that "good Christians" don't have unacceptable impulses and temptations. Mr. Hyde is the hidden half and Dr. Jekyll is the visible half. Hyde isn't hidden to us personally—we all know we have a dual nature. But we hide it in our Christian circles. It's more natural to talk about growth and progress and spiritual victories than of struggles and temptations. We fear what others might think in our relentless quest for approval.

We feel alone, believing most Christians don't struggle as we do. Striving for fellowship often magnifies the duality and sinks the hidden half deeper into the psyche.

But there is hope. There are strategies for dealing with duality. Ironically, one strategy is realizing that duality can never be "fixed." Humans have always had a dual nature, and it is sure to continue as part of the human condition.

A Long History

Duality was evident from the beginning. Fig leaves of shame quickly followed the beauty of a singularly good creation. King David, though a man after God's heart, was plagued by duality. Duality was the cardinal trait of the New Testament Pharisees. Jesus referred to them as whitewashed tombs, clean on the outside but filled with wickedness and evil. Even the Apostle Paul struggled with duality.

> For that which I am doing I do not understand; for I am not practicing what I would like to do, but I am doing the very thing I hate.... For the good that I wish, I do not do; but I practice the very evil that I do not wish.... For I joyfully concur with the law of God in the inner man, but I see a different law in the members of my body, waging war against the law of my mind, and making me a prisoner of the law of sin which is in my members (Rom. 7:15, 19, 22, 23).

Many human conditions have been improved throughout the course of history. I have difficulty imagining life without electricity, toilets, and word processors. Medical advances have prolonged longevity and enhanced the quality of physical well-being. Industrialization has expanded our productivity. But despite our progress, duplicity appears to be timeless. We can't

change the essence of human nature despite our techni-
cal progress. King David's extramarital affair is shock-
ing when we read of it. But a study published in 1983
suggests slightly more than 40% of married adults have
been unfaithful to their spouses.[1] We have not overcome our dual nature despite progress in other areas.

Perhaps our duplicity has not changed throughout
history because it cannot change, it can only be managed. Duality is characteristic of the human condition.

Freaks

Erich Fromm labeled humans the "freaks" of the
universe because, unlike the rest of the animal kingdom, we have rational capacities. Like animals, we
have impulses causing desires for food, sex, pleasure,
avoidance of pain, and so forth, but we also have a
higher nature, allowing us to reason. Impulses to eat
are countered with thoughts about calories or choles-
terol. Impulses of pleasure sometimes oppose attitudes
regarding morality or productivity. Impulse and reason
are often in opposition.

Consider Mike, a happily married business execu-
tive. Mike is committed to his family. He knows that
marital infidelity leads to a host of problems including
lack of trust, communication difficulties, and inse-
curity. He knows these things because he is able to
reason. But Mike also has basic impulses. He is attracted to his wife's close friend Janice. Sometimes
Mike is preoccupied with Janice while sitting at his

1. Thompson, A. P. (1983). Extramarital sex: A review of the research
literature. *Journal of sex research,* 19, 1–22.

desk attempting to complete paperwork. Occasionally he drives by Janice's house on his way home from work and hopes that she is working in the front yard or arriving home at the same time. Mike is distracted. His job performance is suffering; he is more irritable with his children; and his wife wonders what has happened to the marriage. He enjoys the feelings of attraction, but is tired of the struggle. How can he cope?

Mike is a victim of rationality. If he had no ability to reason, he would be driven only by impulse and would experience little or no conflict. But Mike is human, one of Fromm's "freaks," and his rational processes are in conflict with his impulses. He is experiencing the inevitable duality of nature.

It is a basic dichotomy of life. We experience both impulse and rationality, yet they are often incompatible. So we live our lives in conflict: wondering how much to spend on the new car or how fast to drive on the freeway or how much lasagna to take when offered second helpings.

Seeking an Answer

We have developed a good approach to duality—we look for resolution. Many conflicts have good answers, but the conflict of our basic duality has no easy answer. In fact, *looking for ways to eliminate our dual nature makes the duplicity stronger.* The more Dr. Jekyll tried suppressing Mr. Hyde, the more evil and determined Mr. Hyde became.

> . . . because I have been made to learn that the doom and burthen of our life is bound forever on man's shoul-

ders, and when the attempt is made to cast it off, it but
returns upon us with more unfamiliar and more awful
pressure.

Dr. Jekyll

Similarly, if we pretend impulses don't exist, temptation comes in greater force and we are unprepared.
Insisting on finding an easy answer robs us of the rich
learning God intends for us. Groping with duality can
be productive and useful.

Mike can try looking for answers. He might try cold
showers every morning and evening. He might become
more involved in family or religious activities to dis-
tract him from Janice. He might attempt to make
advances toward Janice to satisfy his impulses. But
none of these answers will really resolve the conflict
between his impulse and his rationality. Distraction
techniques may work for a time, but the impulses will
fight back. To fight back the impulses will have to be
stronger. They probably will be. Giving in to the impulses may appear to resolve the conflict, but infidelity
creates scores of new conflicts. The fundamental duality exists. An easy answer does not.

Managing vs. Eliminating Duality

If there is no answer to duality, why read this book?
The key is not *eliminating* duality, but *managing* duality. For example, pretend you're on a diet. After your
chef salad with low-cal Italian dressing the waiter returns with a tray of sumptuous desserts. You have an
impulse to eat dessert but your rational processes are
insisting on abstinence. How likely is it that any kind

of self-management strategy will *eliminate* that conflict? Not very! The most you can hope for is *managing* the conflict. Later that night, as your stomach growls in front of the television set, you recognize both the difficulty of losing weight and the value of self-discipline. Despite your hunger, you feel good about your decision to manage the impulse.

Trying to eliminate duality makes it harder to manage. The converse is also true: managing duality is easier after shedding the unrealistic expectation that it can be eliminated. Conflicts can be growth producing after shedding delusions of finding easy answers.

Suppose Mike concludes that his conflict has no immediate solution. He might begin to look more closely at his experience rather than desperately scrambling for recipe-like answers. In exploring his feelings and investigating his motives he might begin to understand more fully the meaning of marital fidelity, the devastating consequences of infidelity, and the value of commitment to moral standards. He will learn more about grace and love and pain. He will grow.

It is a great paradox. Denying duality makes it grow stronger. Managing duality is growth producing. The goal is not to resolve duality, but to *manage* and *learn* from duality.

2

Life Motives

> ...I was driven to reflect deeply and
> inveterately on that hard law of life, which lies at
> the root of religion and is one of the most
> plentiful springs of distress. Though so profound
> a double-dealer, I was in no sense a hypocrite;
> both sides of me were in dead earnest; I was no
> more myself when I laid aside restraint and
> plunged in shame, than when I laboured, in the
> eye of day, at the furtherance of knowledge or the
> relief of sorrow and suffering....
>
> Dr. Jekyll

The smorgasbord is one of life's great tragedies. The first time through the line I look longingly at delightfully appetizing foods. Unfortunately, I have already filled my plate with the salads that always reside at the beginning of the food line. My only consolation is that I may return as many times as desired. But, as is supposed to happen, I am not hungry after eating twenty-three varieties of salads, and I sit in conflict deciding whether or not to return for that formerly appetizing food. Two opposing forces are operating. One is my memory of the food that looked so good. The other is my brimming stomach, proclaiming the now-aged adage, "I can't believe you ate the whole thing."

Opposing forces are common. We see them in electromagnetic form in general chemistry. They keep us from crossing the red and black connectors when jump-starting the car (the car with the battery we were going to replace last week). Our children struggle for values in the midst of opposing forces of society and home.

Duality also consists of opposing forces. Previous writers have used many different labels for the opposing forces of duality.

Impulsivity

One life motive is *impulse*. Freud called it *ID* or primary process. Jung called it the *shadow*. Paul labeled it *the old self, the sin nature*. Whatever we call it, we can't deny its existence. This is the selfish side of our nature focused on gratifying our needs and desires. In Ephesians 4 we see it equated with greed, sensuality, and impurity. Impulsiveness is in all of us, but its purist form is found in very small children.

When our youngest daughter was less than a year old, I affectionately referred to her as our "ID-KID", because her impulsive nature was so apparent. Megan did whatever she wanted, whenever she wanted. Trying to dissuade her produced an adrenaline-producing scream. Our first two children had been more compliant and my wife, Lisa, and I had earlier agreed that no child of ours would be a screamer. We were wrong. Fortunately (and with a lot of hard work), Megan has developed into a responsive toddler, consisting of much more than mere impulse. Our experience with Megan reflects how fundamental the impulsive nature is. All children are impulsive to some extent, but some are more challenging than others.

Impulsiveness does not disappear after infanthood. Whatever our age, we are inclined to seek pleasure at the expense of others. In junior high I raised my self-esteem by criticizing others. I found endless detail that could be attacked in others, seeking my own impulsive self-satisfaction. They wore the wrong kind of tennis shoes, or their pants were too short, or they rode the cheapest bicycle—whatever! As adults we continue to struggle with impulse. Remember Pastor *A*, Mr. *B*, Mrs. *C*, and Ms. *D*?

Becky was a twenty-eight-year-old woman coming for counseling because of problems she could not define well. Within the first few sessions it became clear that her primary motivation was to seek a psychologist's signature so she could maintain her welfare benefits. She seemed to forget that psychologists cannot prescribe medication, because she frequently asked for codeine. I later discovered Becky was a prostitute, addicted to codeine. She was caught sneaking into the hospital pharmacy to obtain her drugs. Her life was dictated almost solely by impulse.

Becky was obviously motivated by impulse. Other examples of impulsive behavior are more subtle. Impulsiveness is a master of disguise, coming in many forms, some seemingly quite noble. The Pharisees of the New Testament were also ruled by impulse. Several characteristics of an impulsive lifestyle are seen both in Becky and the Pharisees.

Approval seeking. Pharisees loved to stand on the street corners to practice their righteousness. Becky was so desperate for approval that she prostituted herself. Our need for approval is impulsive, often interfering with rightness. Examples are plentiful. Teenage gang members violate the rights of others in order to gain approval from peers. College students violate institutional rules because of peer pressure. Large donations are sometimes given for social recognition and approval.

Rigid thinking. A general rigidity or inflexibility is associated with the impulsive motive. The Pharisees displayed this with pious definitions of righteousness. They were unwilling to accept any other standard, such as that offered by Jesus. Becky's rigid thinking was seen in her single-mindedness. Her life was directed toward obtaining drugs and she was unable to consider other issues.

Defensiveness. Any effort to alter either the Pharisees or Becky resulted in a defensive attack. This is similar to Megan's screaming when we attempted to control her impulses as a one-year-old. The Pharisees often defended themselves by accusing others of blasphemy. Becky defended herself by blaming society for her difficulties. Avoiding responsibility and defensive blaming of others is impulsive behavior.

Pretense. Artificiality abounds in the impulsive person. Becky played a game to get welfare benefits. Pharisees pretended to be righteous but were, in Jesus' words, "white-washed tombs." Impulse is the wedge that creates duality. The greater the impulsive motive, the more duality is present. This is considered more in the next two chapters.

Rationality

The second life motive, *rationality*, is more positive. Although not from a specifically Christian world view, Jung called it *the self-system*, Allport labeled it *proprium-striving*, and Maslow called it a *being-orientation*. The concepts are very similar. This part of our nature seeks truth and understanding. It is metaphysical and depends exclusively on our human ability to reason.

> Then God said, "Let Us make man in Our image, according to Our likeness; and let them rule over the fish of the sea and over the birds of the sky and over the cattle and over all the earth, and over every creeping thing that creeps on the earth. And God created man in his own image, in the image of God He created him; male and female He created them (Gen. 1:26, 27).

God's image has been described in many different ways. Although I don't pretend to understand all of God's image, it seems to me that rationality is part of it. Poet Archibald MacLeish noted "the only thing about a man that is a man is his mind. Everything else you can find in a pig or a horse."

I looked for a better word than *rationality* to capture this second life motive, but I didn't find one. Don't confuse rationality with sterile logic. I'm not suggesting we become like Star Trek's Mr. Spock, having no emotions. Rationality, as I use it, means the capability to analyze experience. Experience includes thought, emotion, and intuition. Carl Jung considered both thinking and feeling to be rational functions. Similarly, Danish theologian and philosopher Søren Kierkegaard observed that thinking was not sufficient for understanding all experience. For example, faith involves more than logic. Rationality must be defined very broadly.

Whereas the impulsive motive is self-centered, the rational motive is truth-centered. It neither exalts nor humiliates self, but rather seeks truth. For example, Pastor *A* is sexually attracted to a member of his congregation. His impulsive motive encourages him to pursue a relationship regardless of morality or else condemns himself as worthless for feeling inappropriate emotions. In either case, the emphasis is on himself (egocentric). His rational motive causes him to explore his feelings so he better understands himself, his conflicts, and God's character. He then is better able to empathize with the conflicts faced by others (truth-centered). The rational motive does not focus on self, but on understanding.

Characteristics of those functioning within this truth-centered framework have been described by personality theorists. In each case the truth-centeredness of Christ's life presents a marked contrast to the ego-centered, impulsive style of the Pharisees.

Acceptance of others. Truth-centered individuals have a remarkable ability to accept others. These persons are not threatened by the strengths of others. Remember the acceptance Jesus had for tax-gatherers? The Pharisees were offended by his willingness to dine with sinners.

Spontaneous. Truth-centered individuals usually function in conventional ways, but are not bound to conventional behaviors. They break the mold when necessary. They have a clear sense of morality but do not have to conform to please others. The Pharisees were angered when Jesus broke the custom by healing a man's hand on the Sabbath. Jesus was being unconventional, but his behavior was both spontaneous and moral. The Pharisees objected because of their rigid—even mindless—conformity to the Old Testament law.

Problem-centered. They have genuine concern for the big problems in life. Truth-centered individuals are concerned about social issues such as hunger, aggression, and prejudice. Again, the life of Christ is marked by concern for the oppressed while the Pharisees often participated in the oppression.

Resistant to criticism. They are not greatly moved either by flattery or criticism. They are more concerned with external issues than self-image. Jesus continued his ministry despite the frequency of ridicule and criticism. Pharisees responded to Jesus' criticism by plotting to destroy him.

Genuineness. Truth-centered individuals lack phoniness. They are comfortable accepting themselves and are willing to show their true selves to others. The Pharisees were the antithesis of genuineness. They performed righteous ceremonies to be noticed. Jesus said that being noticed by others was the full reward for their phony spirituality.

Giving love. They are able to love the essence of another person, regardless of worldly status or posses-

sions. This is the love Christ described in the parable of
the Good Samaritan. In contrast, impulsive forces lead
to a love motivated by meeting one's own needs, such
as the love demonstrated by the Pharisees.

Figure 1 The two motives of personality.

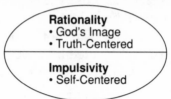

In summary, our impulsive nature leads us to duality. Rationality, God's image in created form, allows
us to understand and manage impulse as we seek
truth. Impulsive motives cause approval seeking, rigidity, defensiveness, and artificiality. Rational motives
cause acceptance of others, spontaneity, problem-
centeredness, resistance to criticism, and genuine loving. The goal of Christian maturity and the goal of
effective counseling are the same: to move from impulsivity to rationality. But a great obstacle stands in the
way of moving toward rationality—an obstacle with
two faces.

3

Two Faces of Impulse

> ...And indeed the worst of my faults was a certain impatient gaiety of disposition, such as has made the happiness of many, but such as I found it hard to reconcile with my imperious desire to carry my head high, and wear a more than commonly grave countenance before the public. Hence it came about that I concealed my pleasures....
>
> Dr. Jekyll

Lori, a young Christian who abandoned social drinking after her conversion, found herself unable to abstain completely. Her willpower occasionally gave way and she binged on alcohol. The next morning's hangover reminded her of her worthlessness and unworthiness. This was such a private part of Lori that we were counseling for many months before she revealed it. Her battle was an impulsive one.

On one hand, Lori craved alcohol. She had learned to enjoy the effects and the taste. On the other hand, Lori believed that good Christians don't use alcohol. So she kept her battle private, not daring to threaten her fragile self-image by revealing her conflict to another. The battle raged!

Lori's situation demonstrates the two sides of impulsivity, the "dark side" and "glossy side." The dark side caused her to drink and enjoy herself. The glossy side caused her to abstain to gain approval from other Christians.

Figure 2 The two faces of impulse.

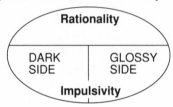

The Dark Side

The dark side of impulse is egocentric, focusing on self. Like Freud's concept of ID, the dark side seeks pleasure and avoids pain. It is irrational and considers none of the constraints of reality.

Is the dark side always evil? No. Although Mike's attraction to Janice is a result of a dark-side impulse, the attraction itself is not evil. But if Mike chooses to respond by engaging in wrongful fantasy or behavior, he has then sinned. The dark side is neither evil nor good, but a vehicle for impulse. Just as temptation is not evil; impulse without immoral action or thought is not evil. This will be considered more later.

The dark side has several distinct characteristics.

Immediate gratification. I had never baked Lisa a birthday cake before. She was gone for a couple hours so I went to the store and picked up a cake mix and a box of frosting. Later, feeling quite domestic, I sat the children on the kitchen counter, pulled the round perfect-looking cake from the oven and began mixing the frosting. I was hungry.

Using my creative genius, I invented an idea for a new style of birthday cake—a square one. Simply by cutting off the sides of the round cake, I could make a square one. Of course the real motivation (and the real genius) was that I could then eat the cut-off sides. The cake was truly delicious though the square cake was smaller than I had anticipated.

If I had ever frosted a cake before I would have realized my folly. I would have realized that frosting does not stick to a crumbly surface. Instead I tried for many frustrating minutes to put frosting over my now-square cake. The cake got smaller and smaller and the frosting became more and more lumpy with crumbs. It eventually looked like a casserole in a seventh-grade-home-economics class. The reality of my failure fell upon me suddenly as my four-year-old daughter looked thoughtfully at the mess and then cautiously asked, "Papa, how many cakes have you made before?" I gave up on my square cake. On my second trip to the store, the clerk assured me that no one could foul up making a cake with a mix. I assured her that I could.

My basic problem was not a culinary deficit, but that I did not delay gratification. I could have waited two hours for dinner. My dark side viewed the cake, assessed the emptiness in my stomach, and created the seemingly genius idea of a square cake. Waiting for dinner was not good enough. I wanted the taste of that cake right then. The dark side hates to wait!

Avoid responsibility. The dark side hates responsibility. To be responsible is to delay pleasure. Most of
the things we do just out of a sense of responsibility are
not pleasant. Some are even mildly painful.

Mowing the lawn is an example. God could have
made lawns that didn't grow. Why didn't he? I hate to
mow the lawn. If my dark side had its way, I would
never mow the lawn.

Jim was a student in one of my college classes. He
was bright, well liked, and had good academic potential. It seemed unusual when he missed three of the
first four days of class. As we talked in my office, he
explained that he was under a lot of stress. His explanation seemed reasonable. Weeks passed, and Jim still
didn't come to class. I assumed he dropped the course
until he showed for the midterm. He failed the test, but
continued to miss class and never picked up his cor-
rected exam. He showed up again for the final and again
failed. The same thing happened the following term
with a different class. Why was Jim in college? Why did
he enroll in classes if he wasn't going to attend?

I suspect Jim had good intentions of coming to class
when he enrolled. But when the alarm rang at 7:30 A.M.,
his dark side captured him. "It's just too early." "You
can get the notes from someone." "You need your
sleep." Jim avoided responsibility and a college di-
ploma.

Aggressiveness. Aggressive impulses come from
the dark side. The human capacity for destruction is
mind boggling. In the name of defense and peace, we
now have the ability to destroy the world over two

dozen times. Fifty-five million people were killed during World War II alone, with Hitler killing up to six thousand Jews per day. Plotless films filled with automatic weapons and needless destruction fill theaters and break box-office records.

These impulses also affect domestic life. Children adeptly bring out aggression in parents. Mothers in average homes speak irritably to children once every two to three minutes. Often parental aggression takes more extreme forms of yelling, harsh discipline, or unnecessary restriction.

Think of the irony of parenting. A twenty-four-year-old is given the responsibility of caring for a new human being. Ecstatic at first, the parents examine the child's fingers and toes over and over. Church members share in the joy and give a baby shower. There are frequent reminders of their sacred responsibility as Christian parents. But soon the ecstasy wears off and there is no real training for dealing with this new child. The child cries for no reason. It is impossible to get a good night's sleep. Husband and wife have less time together and feel as if they need more. The support system at church seems to disappear as the novelty of the new birth subsides. The stress builds, and aggression emerges. It may first be directed toward co-workers or the spouse. Soon it is redirected toward the child. Fortunately, in most cases the impulses are never converted into physical abuse.

The recent publicity of spouse abuse further substantiates the dark side characteristic of aggression. One in ten women will be assaulted by their spouse at some point in their marriage. Those women finally pressing charges will have been attacked an average of thirty-five times! Recent evidence suggests that husbands are also abused by wives at a surprisingly high rate. Domestic aggressiveness is more widespread than most imagine. Aggression results from dark-side impulses being put into action.

Sexual conflicts.   Todd was my second counseling client in my first graduate school practicum. A bright young man with good social skills, he reported having a snake phobia. It was a textbook case. I estimated that six sessions would resolve his problem. My supervisor was less convinced. The sessions went by but Todd did not improve. He seemed to think the treatment was silly, but I kept persevering. Eventually I understood that more than a fear of snakes was bothering Todd. He feared he was homosexual, but couldn't tell me until he knew he could trust me. Since then I have seen many who, like Todd, have major sexual crises. They fear rejection but desperately want help.

It's sometimes awkward to talk about sexuality. Some turn red and change the subject. One cartoon had a grade-school boy whispering to another, "I finally found out what sex is; my sister plays one in the school band." Because of our reticence to discuss sex, we don't share our sexual conflicts with others. We relegate the sexual conflicts to the dark side so nobody can see them.

But sexual conflicts are widespread! In the late 1940s one researcher found that 37 percent of males, like Todd, had experienced a homosexual encounter.[1] Be-

1. Kinsey, A. C., Pomeroy, W. B., and Martin, C. E. (1948). *Sexual behavior in the human male*. Philadelphia: W. B. Saunders.

cause of sampling techniques, the results may have been upwardly biased, but it points to a wide-range sexual confusion, even forty years ago. I've already mentioned a 1983 study showing that over 40% of married adults have been sexually unfaithful to their spouses. Can we even begin to estimate how many others have sexual conflicts with pornography? How many have secret attractions to co-workers causing personal conflict? Sexual conflicts are common.

The Glossy Side

Remember Lori? She struggled with dark-side impulses to drink alcohol. She also had an impulse not to ever drink alcohol because of what others might think. The first impulse is clearly from the dark side. It is an effort to seek pleasure at whatever cost.

The second impulse may, at first, appear to be rational. Lori believed she should never drink alcohol because good Christians don't. A closer look shows very little cerebral functioning involved. Lori didn't choose abstinence from alcohol by careful biblical evaluation. Neither was she abstaining because of concern for social problems caused by alcohol. Just as an animal can learn morality based on avoidance of punishment, Lori had determined not to drink alcohol to avoid disapproval (punishment) from other Christians. This is the *glossy side*, an effort to appear polished and perfect whatever the cost. Notice that both the dark side and glossy side are impulsive and egocentric, focusing only on self.

The similarities between the Pharisees and the impulsive life motive were outlined in chapter 2. Pharisees were strongly influenced by dark-side impulses, but Jesus was more critical of their glossy sides. They invested great effort in polishing and shining their exteriors so others would honor them. Decisions were based on custom and approval seeking rather than rational understanding.

Those with enormous glossy sides often attract large followings. They might even be great leaders of people and great authors because their words and their appearances are so well polished. But behind the words and the appearance there may be little or no truth seeking. Several characteristics identify the glossy side.

Answer-oriented. Convincing students that good counseling is not just giving answers for problems is challenging. Sometimes answers are very useful, but the person who *always* has an answer may drive others away.

Alice confides to her friend Shelly that life has been a struggle lately. Alice feels blue, thinks poorly of herself, and sees very little hope in the future. Shelly listens politely and then says that God causes these things to work together for good and that prayer and Bible study will help Alice regain enthusiasm for life. Alice leaves feeling misunderstood, guilty, and unspiritual.

Shelly's motives were good. She genuinely wanted to help Alice. But her trite answer did not address the depth of depression experienced. It was a recipe answer, lacking a true understanding of the problem.

We all know those who have answers for everything. Very often these answers appear superficial and lacking in insight. Carl Jung wrote of the "Old Wise Man" quality that is seen in individuals who draw great crowds, but have very little to say. Their speech is often a string of clever clichés and well-devised adages. They have glossy exteriors.

The exposure of Jim and Tammy Bakker caused a variety of reactions from Christians. As more and more details became known, the Bakkers' glossy side became apparent. The answers they gave to others were not apparent in their personal lives. Their charismatic style attracted millions of dollars and deep loyalties, but underneath the surface simmered a life of duality and impulse.

As the Bakker scandal was unfolding, another evangelist openly criticized their hypocrisy and sin. Less than one year later, Jimmy Swaggart confessed to his own sexual sin. Swaggart's glossy side glowed during the Bakker scandal but was stripped away as the world watched in February 1988.

Glossy-coated Pharisees probably always had an answer from the law for any question. They had answers for Jesus even when he didn't invite them.

The purpose of always having an answer is probably related to self-esteem. If I have an answer for every question of yours, then I know more than you. That makes me important. My glossy side shines. (Answerism will be considered more in chapter 7.)

Quick to judge. Just as having an answer for every problem builds self-esteem, so does pointing out faults for every problem. What if Shelly told Alice that her depression was the result of sin in her life? Doesn't that sound a lot like the advice of Job's friends? This kind of counsel is not uncommon.

Many authors advocate this perspective. Emotional difficulties, these authors suggest, are a result of sin. If the sin is removed, the problems will go away. These authors are sincere but in my opinion, misguided. Coping with emotional problems is a complicated process of understanding the world more fully, requiring the truth-seeking rational motive. Judging others on a moral level for emotional problems is likely to cause Mr. Hyde to sink deeper into the hidden half. Clients may appear to be better, but only because the duality becomes more disguised.

Shoulds. "Dad, why do I have to pick up the toys in my bedroom?" "Because I said so—just do it!" Does that sound familiar? It is so easy to establish arbitrary authority with children and to quell that very natural desire they have to know why. As a result, we sometimes teach our children that our *shoulds* have no *whys*.

But hold on! Maybe we believe in *shoulds* as our children do. Lawrence Kohlberg and other moral development researchers argue that the majority of adults make moral decisions based upon the letter of the law without considering broader aspects of human welfare. Most define right and wrong with *shoulds* and not with *whys*.

This is exactly what the Pharisees did! They had laws for everything! They insisted the disciples of Jesus refrain from picking a few handfuls of wheat on the Sabbath. I wish Jesus would have asked *why* it was wrong. They probably would have stammered a bit and finally said something like, "because the law says so." Jesus reminded the Pharisees of the Old Testament account of David's eating the sacred bread when he needed food while running from Saul. Jesus made his point well. *Shoulds* are impulsive unless backed up with *whys*. God gives reasons for his requirements in the Bible. We are to obey with or without a reason, as our children are in picking up the toys in their rooms, but Scripture allows us to understand why we are told to behave in prescribed ways. *Whys* move *shoulds* from impulsivity to rationality.

Temptation as evil. If Christians were surveyed, most would say temptation is not a sin. Giving in to the temptation with inappropriate thoughts or actions is a sin. Jesus was tempted (Mark 1:12, 13), yet was without sin. Therefore temptation is not sin. This is a rational argument.

But the glossy side responds quite differently. If we could now take those same Christians and put "guilt-meters" on their foreheads, we might be intrigued by the results. In the presence of temptation, I suspect many of the meters would register significant guilt. The thoughts that produce guilt are predictable. "Good Christians don't have temptations like this." "If I were focusing on the Lord, I wouldn't be noticing attractive men at the office." "If others knew about this temptation, I would be asked to resign from the deacon board." And so on. These thoughts are not based on rational arguments, but on approval seeking and *shoulds*. Because of the glossy side we tend to view the dark side as evil.

I don't see the dark side as evil, but as a vehicle for temptation. Temptation, in turn, can be used for evil or good. If temptation causes sin, then the outcome is clearly evil. But temptation can also be productive. The value of temptation is clearly seen in Scripture:

> Consider it all joy, my brethren, when you encounter various trials, knowing that the testing of your faith produces endurance. And let endurance have its perfect result, that you may be perfect and complete, lacking in nothing (James 1:2–4).

The Greek word translated "trials" in verse two is translated "temptation" in verse thirteen. The source of temptation is internal (vv. 13, 14), from within the dark side of our character, but that temptation can be used to produce growth.

It may seem a trivial distinction to say the dark side is a vehicle rather than intrinsically evil. Actually, it is a very important point. If the dark side is evil, we will respond by trying to eliminate rather than manage it. The result is a battle of impulses as described in the next chapter. *In looking for ways to eliminate our dual nature we make the duplicity stronger.* If the dark side is viewed as a vehicle then our efforts will not be to eliminate it but to manage it and grow in the process.

The Righteousness of the Glossy Side

Just as we tend to view the dark side as evil, we tend to view the glossy side as good. The glossy side endorses a form of righteousness and encourages perfection. Christ also encouraged perfection. But the glossy side is far from righteous because it so centrally focuses on self and not on the broader dimensions of God's truth.

A short time ago, I stumbled across some intriguing research. Church members and those with traditional

Christian beliefs are more racially prejudiced than non-members and those with less traditional beliefs! How can this be? We who speak of the love of Christ, who speak of and hear repeatedly the account of the Good Samaritan, are actually more *prejudiced* than the rest of the population!

But as I read on, I found some additional information. Those who internalize their religious values are less prejudiced than other church attenders. Regular church attenders who view their religious beliefs as fundamental to their entire lives are less prejudiced than irregular attenders and those who see church as a means to an end (such as social activity). It started to make sense.[2]

Some attend church because of glossy-side impulses. They are motivated by social interaction and the personal approval needs the church can meet. I have no objection to church fulfilling this function, but I hope for greater motivation in church attendance. Others attend church because they are seeking truth. They have a desire to learn, to edify others, to understand, and to grow. In sum, the motivation for church attendance can come from either impulsivity or rationality. Those who attend church because of glossy-side impulses are more prejudiced.

Again, the Pharisees are a good example. Their pseudorighteousness was the result of glossy-side impulses. They wanted others to notice their piety and to respect their spiritual positions. But their prejudice

2. Gorsuch, R. L., and Aleshire, D. (1974). Christian faith and ethnic prejudice: A review and interpretation of research. *Journal for the scientific study of religion*, 13, 281–307.

was probably unequaled! They condemned Jesus for interacting with "sinners and tax-gatherers." They had nothing to do with half-breed Samaritans or the Gentiles.

True righteousness is not motivated by the glossy side. Pseudo-righteousness is a self-centered form of piety far from God's notion of spirituality. True spirituality focuses on truth rather than self.

In the past three chapters I have argued that two forces are fundamental to the human condition: rationality and impulsivity. Moreover, the impulsive has two sides: the dark side and the glossy side. Both impulses are focused on self and neither involve a deep search for truth. Having defined these components of personality, the dynamics of duality can now be considered. Because the dark and glossy sides are in opposition to one another, the stage is set for a battle of impulses.

4

Battle of Impulses

> ...All things therefore seemed to point to this;
> that I was slowly losing hold of my original and
> better self, and becoming slowly incorporated
> with my second and worse.
>
> Dr. Jekyll

Jekyll was losing control. Hyde was taking over. The impulsive was growing stronger and the rational was shrinking in defeat. *Neurotic anxiety* is how Freud described the fear of the dark side taking over the rational. Many have the fear but few verbalize it. Neurotic anxiety causes us to attempt in futility to get rid of the dual nature that can never really be eliminated. This fear often pushes us into a battle of impulses—an ineffective struggle that defies rationality and ends in personal defeat and despair.

Destroying the Dark Side:
An Impossible Task

Neurotic anxiety was Luke Skywalker's problem in Episode V of the Star Wars series, *The Empire Strikes Back*. The great (but funny-looking) Jedi master, Yoda, was training young Skywalker to become a Jedi knight. Luke feared that the evil side of the force would become too strong if not destroyed immediately. But his style was impulsive. Skywalker sensed evil in a nearby cave and approached the cave with caution. Yoda called out, "Your weapons, you will not need them." Luke ignored Yoda and entered the cave with his light sword at his side. Suddenly the evil Darth Vader seemed to appear in the cave. The sword fight was brief as Luke lopped off Vader's head. But as the black helmet lay on the ground, Skywalker's own face gradually appeared beneath the face shield. Had Luke killed part of himself?

The potential for evil is dissonant for us as it was for Skywalker in the creative fantasy of George Lucas. We want to destroy evil and live in peace. We want to remove temptation and live in clarity. So we take up our swords impulsively to purge evil by destroying it. Yet, the evil we seek to destroy is part of our very identity. In the process we short-circuit growth and escalate neurotic anxiety.

What did Yoda have in mind when he told Skywalker not to take his weapon? Perhaps Yoda knew that the evil Luke was about to confront was his own. It could not be destroyed with weapons; it could only be understood.

So it is with us. In fear that our dark side will take over, we seek to destroy it. We swing our weapons impulsively. We use the arbitrary *shoulds*, the easy answers, and the judgmental perspectives of the glossy side. We strike down our dark side and feel immediate relief. But gradually we become aware that we have attempted to eradicate a part of ourselves which can never stay dead but only return with greater determination. Jan's case illustrates this.

Jan was an attractive thirty-year-old accountant successfully employed by a large manufacturing company. With dismay she recognized her attraction toward Tom, a co-worker, as more intense than feelings toward other colleagues. When Tom revealed his attraction to her, Jan's confusion intensified. Because she was married, she felt guilty, and tried to eliminate her feelings. Not only were her efforts futile, they seemed counterproductive. The more she tried to remove Tom from her mind, the more preoccupied with him she became. In desperation she sought the advice of her pastor. She was advised to remove herself from the situation and avoid further exposure to Tom, which meant quitting her job. Armed with new impulsive zeal, Jan promptly resigned her position and began looking for another accounting job. When Tom called, she said that she was changing her life and would prefer that he not contact her.

Several weeks later, Jan arrived with her husband for the first counseling session. During those intervening weeks, she had lost control. Convinced that she could no longer resist the temptation, she called Tom and told him that she was ready to leave her husband. A brief affair followed, but both Tom and Jan knew that it could never work. After attempting suicide, Jan was found by her husband and taken to a nearby hospital. Following her discharge, Jan came for counseling.

Jan's situation illustrates the battle of impulses. The dark side encouraged her to pursue an extramarital relationship. Armed with easy answers the glossy side condemned her for even feeling the temptation. Intensity escalated when Jan decided not to work at the same place as Tom. The glossy side had responded decisively to the neurotic anxiety. But the dark side fought back, and ultimately Jan left her husband. Her guilt intensified as the glossy side again gained control and suicide became an attractive option for escape. When aware of her duality she tried to conquer it with counterimpulses. But such efforts only escalated the battle and left her in defeat and despair.

What might have happened if Luke left his weapons at the door of the cave as Yoda suggested? What might have happened if Jan had refused to fight impulse with impulse? She might have acknowledged the original attraction as impulse caused by her inevitable dual nature and attempted to understand it from a rational perspective. In trying to understand her feelings, she might have discussed it from the very beginning with a supportive friend. If these efforts did not lead to understanding, she might have sought counseling to better analyze her feelings. In the process she might have developed greater personal insight and an anticipation for future conflicts. *The very experience with duality that became a battleground for Jan could have been a positive opportunity for spiritual and personal growth.*

Synergism

When prescribing barbiturates, physicians warn that these drugs not be used in conjunction with alcohol. The two drugs are synergistic—the two drugs combined are far more dangerous than either drug consumed separately. I am convinced that the glossy side and the dark side are also synergistic. The combination of the two results in a battle with duality of far greater intensity than if either was present without the other.

The dark side evokes the glossy side. To understand the synergism between the two sides of impulse, it is useful to recognize the tendency for dark-side impulses to evoke glossy-side impulses. It is in the "dark room" that the glossies are developed.

As a conservative Christian from a small town, I was overwhelmed by the culture shock when I first went away to a secular college. I was confronted with new temptations on a regular basis, including sexual temptation. During my freshman year two men on my floor brought several pornographic magazines into the dorm lounge. While the others sat around looking at the magazines, I sat reading my chemistry book. On the outside I looked like the steady Christian they had grown to respect. Actually I wanted to see the photos. Morality had little to do with my decision to keep reading my chemistry book. If I had gone over and looked at the magazines, they would have realized I wasn't as pure as they thought. My glossy side would have been tarnished. My decision was not made on a rational basis, even though it was a good one. The glossy side dictated the impulsive decision.

Later, as I was driving by the local convenience store, I suddenly felt the impulse to stop and buy one of those magazines for myself. But almost as quickly, a counter-impulse came from the glossy side. "What if somebody saw you buying that magazine?" "What if word spread around campus?" "You have a reputation to maintain." The dark-side impulses evoked the glossy side.

I now have more autonomy than I did as a college freshman, and it would be quite easy for me to buy a pornographic magazine without anyone recognizing me. Fortunately, my motives have changed from impulsive to rational in this area. I am increasingly aware of the negative consequences of pornography. I have seen the slavery that results, the relationships it affects, and the lack of trust it produces.

When we are tempted to sin, however, we do not always think immediately of how we might appear to others. Alternatively, we might be overwhelmed by a sense of comparison. "A good Christian would never do something like I've just done." "If others knew what I was really like, they would have nothing to do with me." Such comparison thoughts float freely through the mind of a defeated Christian. They are glossy thoughts developed in the "dark room."

Jan's example is a good one. Her guilt developed from her attraction for Tom. The more she was attracted, the more guilty she felt when they were apart. Deciding to take another job was a way to cope with the guilt. As the attraction built, the guilt grew stronger. Of course her guilt became most intense after the brief affair. As with Dr. Jekyll, suicide seemed the only way to cope with massive self-condemnation.

You might be thinking that guilt was appropriate in this case because Jan had sinned. Christian psychologist Bruce Narramore makes a useful distinction between guilt and constructive sorrow in his book *No Condemnation*. Guilt is a feeling of self-condemnation focused on personal failures. Constructive sorrow, in contrast, does not focus on self but rather on grace. This distinction fits well into the model presented in this book. Guilt originates from impulsivity, focusing on self, and is therefore egocentric. Constructive sorrow originates from rationality. It is centered not on self but on the broader truths of God, violation of his principles, and his forgiving grace.

Most of us in a situation like Jan's would feel guilt rather than constructive sorrow. We would focus on our own failure rather than on the violations of God's commandments and the glories of God's grace. The dark side evokes the glossy side, and guilt inevitably results.

The glossy side evokes the dark side. Lucretius warned that "Such evil deeds could religion prompt." Just as the impulses of the dark side evoke the guilt of the glossy side, the unrealistic demands of the glossy side evoke the urges of the dark side. Thus, one impulse fuels the other, and the battle of impulse rages on.

Paul described the Old Testament law as good because it identified sin. But Paul also noted that the law is a catalyst of sin.

> But sin, taking opportunity through the commandment, produced in me coveting of every kind; for apart from the Law sin is dead. And I was once alive apart from the Law; but when the commandment came, sin became alive, and I died; and this commandment, which was to result in life, proved to result in death for me; for sin, taking opportunity through the commandment, deceived me, and through it killed me (Rom. 7:8–11).

The law didn't cause evil, but rather sin working through the format of the law. The *shoulds* of the law evoked hedonistic impulses within Paul, and he experienced the battle with duality he described later in the same chapter. Without the law, the evil desires would have been more manageable.

If the law, being good, caused dark-side impulses, how much more do unnecessary glossy-side impulses evoke temptation? Because Christians at Colossae were being exposed to many unnecessary rules, Paul described the excessive restriction of asceticism. "Do not handle, do not taste, do not touch!" (Col. 2:21). Paul concluded that such glossy rules are of "no value against fleshly indulgence" (v. 23).

Many restrictions in modern Christianity resemble asceticism much more than the law. They are unnecessary restrictions without biblical support. Many Christians were traditionally taught that alcohol, dancing, movies, and playing cards are unspiritual and should be completely avoided. In Paul's words, these rules are of "no value against fleshly indulgence." Often those exposed to the most severe rules become the most severe rebels.

In walking across a college campus recently I found myself strolling on the grass instead of the sidewalk. Groundskeepers would have been upset had they seen me, but I justified my action since there was no sign prohibiting me from walking on the grass. Do you see the irony? If I had never in my whole life seen a KEEP OFF THE GRASS sign, I would probably always walk on the sidewalk because I'm smart enough to know that walking on the grass could damage the lawn. But since I frequently see such signs, I feel justified to walk on the grass when the sign is absent. Rules work the same way as KEEP OFF THE GRASS signs.

These are examples of synergism. The *shoulds* of the law or asceticism represent the glossy side. The hedonistic struggles described by Paul represent the dark side. The glossy side of the law did not cause the dark side in Paul, but it evoked the dark side. Similarly, the intensity of Jan's attraction for Tom was actually stronger because she used counterimpulses from the glossy side to deal with her feelings.

But the battle of impulses is unnecessary. Chapter 8 of Romans explains how Christ fulfilled the law and removed the *shoulds* that lead to condemnation. Conflicts of duality will continue but the mind will be set on the spirit of life and peace and not on the fleshly struggle for acceptability. A rational striving toward God's truth will replace the impulsive battle focused on self-perfection. If Jan would have accepted her attraction to Tom and attempted to learn from her feelings, she might have grown spiritually. If she had made a rational decision to remain faithful despite her attraction for Tom, she might have come to better understand the concept of God's grace. (This understanding of God's grace will be considered more in a later chapter.)

Going in Circles

Brenda, an attractive young woman with a good job and a successful social life, appeared to have everything. But in therapy she admitted her disease of bulimia. Her obsession for food was enormous. She could eat an entire pizza, a half-gallon of ice cream, a loaf of bread, and a jar of applesauce—and still desire to eat more. She would have done well to follow Miss Piggy's advice to never eat more than you can lift.

During the first part of treatment, it was easy to see when Brenda had binged during the week. During those weeks she would come for her appointment and announce that she no longer needed my assistance. She now had enough willpower to make it on her own, she claimed. On one occasion she described this willpower as a solid rock in her soul. I didn't believe her. I thought she was feeling guilty for binging and her guilt was bringing out the so-called willpower. The dark side had evoked the glossy side.

The willpower would usually last between two days and two weeks. She would eat sparingly like the proverbial rabbit. Because she had to shed the pounds she gained during the binge, she would weigh every ounce of food with great caution. The glossy side was strong during these periods.

But no one can eat alfalfa sprouts and celery forever. At last Brenda's glossy side would give way to the dark side and another binge would result. Again, she would feel great willpower and assure me this was the last binge.

Brenda's battle was a battle of the impulses. The impulse to eat evoked the impulse to be perfect. The impulse to be perfect evoked the impulse to eat. The impulses were synergistic. The battle raged on.

As with most bulimics, Brenda's problem began in childhood. The oldest daughter of an alcoholic, she learned early the potential damage of the dark side. She often heard the tirades and felt the physical abuse of her intoxicated father. She decided, in her young mind, to avoid the dark side at all cost. She would live her life in total control. But total control is impossible because we all have a dark side. Brenda tried to hide hers but the result was a cycle of eating and starving, hedonism and guilt, dark side and glossy side.

My efforts focused on helping Brenda see that she could never be perfect—that she will continue to overeat on occasion. We tried to look closely at her binges as learning experiences. At first she resisted. She believed she could not learn from her great sin. She had to be perfect. Over time Brenda began to see that perfection in eating was not the goal. She began to learn from her failures and her goals of perfection were eliminated. Is it surprising that her obsessions to overeat were reduced as she removed herself from the battle of impulses?

As the battle of impulses rages, we can become fixated in the impulsive mode. We might expend all our efforts to conquer the dark side or to overcome the oppression of the glossy side. As the battle continues, a wall builds between the impulsive and the rational and our energies are invested in impulses. But as we force ourselves into rationality—as we begin to look for truth and understanding—the battle ceases. As Brenda began to understand her problem from a larger perspective, the problem became manageable.

The continuing battle of impulses is devastating. Over time, a chronic sense of guilt sets in. Albert Ellis, a well-respected psychologist, concluded that religion is the source of mental illness. He based this on observing ways religious individuals react to sin. The self-condemnation and destructive patterns of thought are hard to deny. They are effects of the battle. Another result can be a pervasive passivity in life. Battles seem to rage out of control, eventually leaving their victims with a sense of helplessness. Erich Fromm identified the goal of organized religion to be powerlessness. The consequences of the battle often affect our self-esteem, our relationships, and our views of God and others in authority. Indeed, it is not the duality of our nature causing the most problems for us as Christians, but rather the impulsive battles from our own efforts to eliminate the duality.

**Figure 3 The battle of impulses.
Rationality is walled off as the battle rages.**

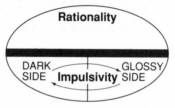

Television Evangelists and
Battles of Impulse

"I know that so many would ask, 'Why?' 'Why?' I have asked myself that ten thousand times through ten thousand tears. Maybe Jimmy Swaggart has tried to live his entire life as though he was not human."

When Jimmy Swaggart spoke these words at the Family Worship Center in Baton Rouge, Louisiana, on February 21, they were lost in the swirl of the emotion. But they may have been his most important words because they hint at the cause of Swaggart's sin and the falling of other church leaders and television evangelists to battles of impulse.

Maybe Jimmy Swaggart has tried to live his life as though he is not human. Maybe he thought his followers expected him to transcend human weakness. Maybe they did. Consider the pressures faced by television evangelists. Each of these pressures adds to glossy-side impulses.

First, television evangelists face demands for perfection. Jesus bluntly exhorted his followers to be perfect as God is perfect (Matt. 5:48), so how could Swaggart's desire to be perfect have contributed to his sin? In a day when we expect polished appearances from our leaders—complete with expensive pinstripes, well-polished shoes, and styled hair—it is easy to confuse *being* perfect with *appearing* perfect, the glossy side.

Second, we expect our leaders to have answers. Many times their answers are good and useful, helping their followers. Unfortunately, answers aren't always personally helpful. Some answers come more from glossy-side impulses than rational understanding. Many people marvel that Swaggart taught that all psychological problems could be solved through Scripture while he himself suffered from an addictive sexual behavior. Consistent with his teaching, he tried to solve his own problem through prayer and Scripture.

Third, our leaders are exposed to careful public scrutiny. How many times did Jimmy Swaggart wonder if his sins would someday be publicly revealed? How many nights did Jim Bakker lay awake wondering what would come of his past extramarital affair? For Swaggart, Bakker, and other fallen leaders, their mistakes became public as their private sins were broadcast in our living rooms. Other church leaders are less exposed but equally tainted with sin.

Fourth, our pastors don't have pastors. We look to our leaders for spiritual strength but often they have nowhere to turn for their own sustenance. Especially after he condemned Bakker's infidelity, Swaggart could not risk revealing his problem to a colleague because of the threat of his problem becoming public. So Swaggart struggled on his own and lost.

Our television evangelists face the same pressures Dr. Jekyll faced in Robert Louis Stevenson's classic. They have an image to uphold; an image perpetuated by public expectations and high personal demands. Because of the pressure, some evangelists try to live their lives as though they aren't human and end up demonstrating to all that they are very human. The glossy side evokes the dark side. The dark side evokes the glossy side.

Summary

Before moving on to some of the traditional ways of coping with duality, let's briefly summarize the personality model described in these chapters.

1. *There is a fundamental human duality.* As humans we have both impulsive capacity and rational capacity. Impulsive motives focus on self whereas rational motives focus on truth. Since this duality is fundamental to the human condition it can never be removed, and self-efforts to do so will result in failure.

2. *Impulsive capacities come in two forms.* Self-focus can take many forms, but can be categorized as two sides of impulse. The dark side consists of impulses to obtain pleasure and minimize pain. Still focusing on self, the glossy side consists of impulses to gain approval and to be blameless in the eyes of others. Pharisees were good examples of glossy-side impulse.

3. *When faced with temptation, we often try to eliminate duality.* Because of the dissonance of duality, we often attempt to remove it. We do this by mindlessly attacking our temptations with impulses from our glossy side. But these attempts to remove duality actually make it worse by creating an internal battle of impulses.

4. *An impulsive battle results.* As we use our weapons of impulse, temptation actually grows stronger. The stronger the temptations, the more we try to destroy them with easy answers, *shoulds* and self-condemnation. The battle escalates and continues to focus on self because of its impulsive nature. Only when we are able to view temptation and conflict from a truth-centered perspective that transcends an emphasis on self can we grow from the experience.

5

Hiding Hyde

> Many a man would have even blazoned such
> irregularities as I was guilty of; but from the high
> views that I had set before me, I regarded and hid
> them with an almost morbid sense of shame. . . .
>
> Dr. Jekyll

For nine months we eagerly anticipated the arrival of our first child. But in the midst of a humid Tennessee summer and a thirty-three-hour labor, a sense of hopelessness contaminated the anticipation. After a full day of contractions, Lisa and I began to cry as we discussed the frustration of seeing almost no progress. The tears came freely, providing a brief reprieve.

Our tears were useful. Crying didn't change the realities of a prolonged labor, but it helped us cope with the battle. Like aspirin for a toothache, the tears relieved immediate tension, causing Lisa to regain strength for the final ten hours.

Coping with the battle of impulses is often similar. Palliative strategies remove us from the intensity of the conflict for a short while, but the battle continues. Many coping strategies, like crying, give temporary relief but don't resolve the problem.

Palliative coping strategies are good for temporary conflicts or battles. They serve as distractors and allow much needed relief. However, palliative coping strategies are not sufficient for ongoing conflicts. Although they provide immediate relief, they don't lead to long-term resolution. For example, crying about long-standing financial problems may feel good, but it won't help resolve the money problems.

This is the difference between Lisa's labor and the battle of impulses. Lisa's labor had an ending point, making palliative coping strategies useful. After our daughter was born, the battle was over. Palliative coping was fine because she just needed to cope for several hours until the birth was accomplished. Battles of impulse last a lifetime. There is no immediate end point, making palliative coping strategies ineffective and counterproductive.

In the next four chapters, we will explore palliative coping strategies used to conquer the battle of impulses. These strategies produce immediate relief, but are eventually self-defeating, resulting in shallow spirituality and unnecessary symptoms of stress. One ineffective coping strategy is *hiding Hyde, pretending the dark side isn't there.*

Persona

A *persona* was a mask worn by actors in early theater. Carl Jung appropriately used the term to label the part of personality that is shown to the world. By showing the persona we hide the dark side (Jung called the dark side the "shadow"). We hide our self-serving impulses and display what we think others will like to see.

I recently learned of a professor at a well-respected Christian college (not the one at which I teach) who gave a female student an A only after she agreed to sleep with him. Another professor at the same college left his wife and moved to another state with one of his students. This is probably not what you expect from Christian college professors. Why not?

College professors have a specific persona. We present ourselves as dignified, controlled, and intellectual. Showing our dark side would be tantamount to admitting defeat as a scholar. We must be superrational at all times, but lurking under the surface of wisdom is the dark side, the shadow. The persona covers the dark side.

We see something similar with Christian leaders. In my counseling I frequently learn of situations involving the immorality of a pastor, a deacon, or an elder. Church leaders have specific personas that cover up their dark sides.

Figure 4 The dark side is suppressed in Hiding Hyde.

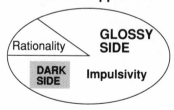

Hiding the dark side allows immediate relief. If we showed our dark side to others, we would only invoke their judgment—so we keep it to ourselves. But privacy can be extended too far. By not acknowledging the dark side—even to God—battles and temptations are magnified and often germinate into sin. Privacy that once produced relief now evolves into neurotic anxiety.

Development

How do we learn to hide the dark side? It probably begins very early. Jerry had been depressed for several months. He came for counseling in desperation, having contemplated suicide. At first it was difficult to empathize with Jerry, an overweight, seemingly apathetic man.

Cognitive therapy, my standard approach to depression, didn't work with Jerry. He twisted my statements into arguments. Arguing is not the point of counseling. Why wasn't he doing better?

On the advice of a colleague, I began exploring Jerry's childhood more carefully. Several sessions later I began to understand Jerry's problem. With tears flowing freely he related his earliest memory. He remembered sitting on the living-room couch listening to his mother say, "I hate you, I hate you, I wish you never were born!" Jerry couldn't remember the act of disobedience, but he could remember his mother's hostile reaction. As Jerry described his memory, I became profoundly aware of my insensitivity. This man whom I had judged as unmotivated and apathetic was actually a victim of a tragic social crime. He was emotionally charred as a child and was living behind the prison bars of his scarred memory.

A string of these parental tirades became apparent as we probed further into childhood. When Jerry acted defiantly or irresponsibly, his mother became enraged and resorted to verbal abuse. He grew to feel alone and inadequate. Jerry thought himself the worst of all children and the worst of all humans. Because of these feelings of inadequacy, he hid his dark side so deeply that even he could not recognize it.

Jerry illustrates how hiding Hyde is learned. Children reveal their dark sides. In response they hear judgment. They then hide the dark side to avoid judgment, and a private struggle results.

But developing duality is more subtle than the extreme example of Jerry. Children do not discriminate well between immoral acts and irresponsible acts. So they try to hide all behaviors that have negative outcomes. In practicing the administration of a psychological test with my four-year-old daughter, I asked what to do if she broke something that belonged to a neighbor. Her answer was quick and serious: "Hide it." One little boy explained to his parents that he was counting sheep when one of them wet his bed. We chuckle at his effort to hide an accidental behavior.

Children spill milk, break dishes, and accidentally hurt playmates. It is a part of childhood. Punishment is not appropriate. Punishing a child for accidental damage communicates that absolute perfection is the only acceptable standard. The gulf between the dark side and the glossy side grows bigger, and the child becomes convinced that every negative aspect of personality must be hidden, whatever the cost.

I spoke harshly to my three-year-old when she wiped her runny nose with her grilled cheese sandwich. But I had been attempting to teach her for weeks to *wipe* her nose instead of continually sniffing. She was not being defiant. She was being partially obedient. When I spoke harshly, I taught her that even unintentional mistakes are unacceptable and must be hidden.

Psychologists Pat Fallon and Marie Root have identified the "perfect family" constellation. Perfect families emphasize excellence, achievement, and appearance. Others look to perfect families and marvel at how well the children behave and how polished they look. The parents emphasize the importance of appearance and demand high standards of academic accomplishment. Children from perfect families, according to Fallon and Root, often fail to develop a sense of personal identity. Efforts to maintain perfection will ultimately fail and, because they lack identity, these children often rebel. It is a quiet rebellion to maintain the appearance of the family, but it is severe. Fallon and Root note the connection between perfect families and eating disorders such as bulimia and anorexia. Hidden substance abuse and promiscuity are other forms of quiet rebellion.[1]

At a recent family camp, I almost immediately noticed the glossy side of one man. Almost everything he said, in meetings and on the activity field, was carefully designed to display personal perfection. He extended his perfection demands to his family. He talked of his commitment to their spiritual development and his interest in their schooling. But we saw a side of his children that he could not see. Lisa taught his youngest in a morning class and had more difficulty controlling her behavior than any other child. His oldest child enjoyed playing with our oldest, Danielle. Once Dan-

---

1. Fallon, Pat, and Root, Marie (1986). Eating disorders: Practical approaches to treatment. Workshop presented February 15, Portland, Ore.

ielle came with her playmate and asked if she could go play in a distant playground. After we denied the request (a meal was approaching), Danielle's friend asked with disgust in her voice, "Why did you ask her?" The seeds of duality had been sown and fertilized in this man's daughters. He demanded the perfection of the glossy side but his children only delivered perfection in his presence. Their behavior elsewhere was far from perfect.

Social Alignment

Social pressure reinforces the tendency to hide the dark side. In most social situations, we tend to show only our acceptable attributes and hide our dark sides, as indicated in Figure 5.

When we see others in a social setting, we see what they want us to see. We rarely see dark-side qualities in others unless revealed in a moment of frustration or extreme temptation. Sometimes we conclude that others do not have dark sides because we so rarely see the weaknesses of others. When we do see the dark side of another, we are so shocked that we respond reflexively. Although less publicized than the Bakker and Swaggart scandals, a sincere Christian leader recently resigned his ministry position when a sin from his past became known. He knew how Christians would respond. It is right to expect purity in our Christian leaders, but our shock reaction to sin is sometimes excessive. Tragically, his ministry can never be the same. If we allowed it, we could learn many lessons from sincere Christians who have remorsefully acknowledged their errors. Instead we banish them from leadership. God uses broken people when we allow him to. Remember King David.

Of course there are those who seem to show their dark sides without remorse. They appear to have no hesitations or regrets about living in open sin. They apply a different coping strategy to be considered in a later chapter. Typically we don't find them in our Christian social circles. Perhaps we are more inclined to hide our dark side among Christians.

Figure 5 We align ourselves socially so others can see our rationality and our glossy sides, but not our dark sides.

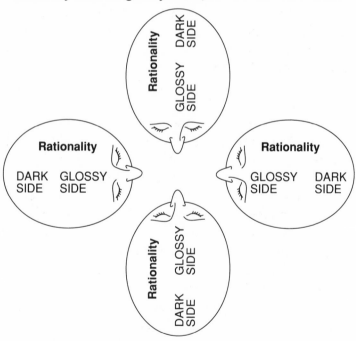

Just as dark-side impulses evoke glossy-side impulses within an individual, dark-side impulses in one person evoke glossy-side impulses in others. When someone dares to admit dark-side impulses, others often respond with judgment and easy answers. One Sunday a young man admitted a problem with anger at a church I was visiting. He acknowledged getting so angry that he wanted to throw things at family members. I appreciated his honesty, but it was quickly punished. A church leader provided him with the answer to his problem: more Bible study. Perhaps the advice was right, but it was insensitive timing. This young man expressed a dark-side impulse, making himself vulnerable, and the response was an easy answer that served to elevate the self-image of the advice giver. The dark side of one evoked the glossy side of another.

I'm not suggesting we totally disclose ourselves to everyone we know. If you revealed everything about your hidden half to casual acquaintances, you might be socially ostracized. Appropriate self-disclosure will be considered more in chapter 10. I'm not condemning our patterns of social alignment, but rather pointing out their role in maintaining duality.

Not only do we hide our dark sides, we often find subtle ways of magnifying our accomplishments. The following anecdote has been going the rounds:

> A man in the dress business called a friend, also in the dress business, and asked him how things were going. "Couldn't be better," answered the friend. "Even with the recession, our sales are up forty percent. My son, the lawyer, just won a big case, and his fee was a million dollars. My other son, the surgeon, was nominated for the Nobel Prize in medicine...."

"I'll phone back later," the caller interrupted. "I didn't know you had someone with you."

Why do we emphasize our accomplishments? Probably because of self-esteem needs. We want others to think highly of us. Sometimes we disguise our boasting because outward arrogance evokes the judgment of others. The glossy side wants the approval of others.

One friend in graduate school was an outstanding student, clearly the "most likely to succeed." Although I didn't realize it at the time, his success threatened me. When around Charlie I found myself dropping subtle hints about my successes. We spent most of our time together talking about the articles I was publishing or progress on my dissertation. Rarely did we talk about Charlie. My glossy side monopolized conversations because of my desire for his approval. If I was really as competent as I wanted to appear to Charlie, I would be a full professor at Harvard by now!

Social alignment results in amplifying our successes and minimizing our dark-side impulses. We begin to believe others do not struggle with the dark side because of social-alignment tendencies. They appear to be successful and without conflict. Their lives appear to be in order with no hint of aggressive impulses or sexual conflicts. Feelings of aloneness and guilt result.

What an irony! We struggle personally with dark-side impulses, but assume others don't because they don't reveal their dark sides any more than we do. Stated in overgeneralized terms, everyone has a dark side but no one knows it.

Results of Hiding Hyde

Hiding the dark side is a palliative coping strategy. It provided immediate relief for Jerry as he coped with the crises of childhood and his mother's disapproval. It relieved Dr. Jekyll who could lead his respectable life and hold his head high in the absence of Mr. Hyde. But the long-term results are often maladaptive.

Conformity and aloneness. Hiding our dark side creates conflict. Externally, we conform to others because we long to be accepted. But internally, we feel alone because we don't see a dark side in other Christians.

In the movie *Taps*, Timothy Hutton leads a group of adolescents at a military school who have decided to defend their institution from being closed by state authorities. The boys find automatic weapons in the school arsenal as the potential for danger becomes apparent. The next night one boy slips over the school fence to escape the danger. The next morning, Hutton calls all the boys together and announces that anyone who wants to leave is free to go. The boys all stand at attention. No one moves. No one wants to be different! Finally, one brave student drops his rifle and walks conscientiously out the gate to safety. As he leaves, others begin filing out. A few at first, then dozens leave the cause for safety.

This scene clearly portrays the need for conformity. None of the boys dared be the first to leave, but once one left justification to leave extended to many. No one wants to be different. We want to fit in with others. We appear weak when we reveal our dark sides to other Christians, so we often conform by hiding Hyde.

Yet as we conform with our behavior, we often feel alone in our personal struggles.

Guilt.   Debbie gazed out over the city from her hillside pedestal of stone—her spot of refuge from the demands of life. This night she looked wistfully at the knife representing escape from her guilt. Slowly she pressed the blade against the flesh of her arms and watched it carve a shallow slice. Again and again she repeated the motion, until her arms streamed with beads of red. Suicide was not her goal. Debbie sought to punish herself in response to overwhelming feelings of guilt.

The next week in counseling, Debbie told me she had again given in to the urge to harm herself. It was not the first time. The scars on her wrists told the story.

As Debbie and I met for the next year and a half, she discussed her tremendous sense of guilt many times. She seemed unable to believe that God could accept her. She felt unworthy and hopeless.

Debbie's impulses were too troubling for her to discuss, even after a year of counseling. Revealing her dark side, she believed, would unleash all the power of evil in her life. She had to keep the door closed to that part of her life. But I could see her impulses as if the door was wide open. At times she seemed to want me to know because she covered them with such shallow disguises. Her secret impulses were not unusually morbid or disgustingly sick, but she protected them with all her emotional strength.

Because others hid their dark sides from Debbie, she became convinced hers was unforgivable. A guilt that stifles all joy overcame her. She knew about her sin, but she wasn't experiencing the grace that removes guilt.

Most guilt does not approach the magnitude of Debbie's. Nonetheless, it commonly blocks the experience of God's grace. We find ourselves lacking in comparison to others. Because our attention is focused impulsively toward ourselves and our guilt, we then miss the greatness of grace that we can only see by looking at God.

Sin. Earlier in the chapter I stated that showing our dark side to others often results in evoking their glossy sides. The church leader's reaction to the young man admitting his impulses of anger illustrates this tendency. But the plot is more complicated. Admitting temptation evokes judgment in others, and judgment of others, in turn, evokes sin in us. It becomes a vicious cycle. Just as the law evoked sin before the age of grace (Romans 7), judgment from others creates a desire to sin.

This sounds more complicated than it is. I become very vulnerable when I risk sharing my dark side. If I get judgment in response, I will feel greater guilt and will be more convinced that I am the only one who struggles with a dark side. Guilt may be motivating for a short while, but it usually backfires in time. The dark side sinks further into seclusion and duality escalates. The next time I am alone in a situation with temptation, I am more likely to stumble because the rational resources for dealing with temptation have been separated by the growing gulf of duality.

Based on this analysis, it is not surprising that a study presented at a conference I recently attended indicated that those with fundamental religious beliefs have personalities with greater propensity for alcoholism than those with other beliefs. Rather than serving as a rational resource, our faith can become an agent of judgment and self-condemnation—one that escalates duality and increases our inclination toward sin. We might easily reason, "because I have taken a drink I have already sinned, so I might as well continue since I've already blown it."

Hiding Hyde is a palliative coping strategy. The immediate relief it provides from social judgment is soon replaced with aloneness, guilt, or sin.

> If we say that we have no sin, we are deceiving ourselves, and the truth is not in us. If we confess our sins, He is faithful and righteous to forgive us our sins and to cleanse us from all unrighteousness. If we say that we have not sinned, we make Him a liar, and His word is not in us (1 John 1:8–10).

6

Hiding Jekyll

... There was something strange in my sensations, something indescribably new, and, from its very novelty, incredibly sweet. I felt younger, lighter, happier in body; within I was conscious of a heady recklessness, a current of disordered sensual images running like a mill race in my fancy, a solution of the bonds of obligation, an unknown but not an innocent freedom of the soul. I knew myself, at the first breath of this new life, to be more wicked, tenfold more wicked, sold a slave to my original evil; and the thought, in that moment, braced and delighted me like wine....

Dr. Jekyll

Bumper stickers are good thermometers to measure the climate of society. Sometime between the peace stickers of the sixties and the No Nuke stickers of the eighties, it was common to see the adage, IF IT FEELS GOOD, DO IT. It's an interesting philosophy, but it doesn't take a great mind to realize that it isn't very practical. One man displaying such a bumper sticker was rammed from behind while waiting at a traffic light. The driver of the assaulting car shrugged and casually remarked, "It felt good."

Sin Solution

After some initial battles with impulse, some decide to abandon traditional morality and seek pleasure. If it feels good, they do it. They abandon the rational life motive and cover up the glossy side. They hide Dr. Jekyll and allow Mr. Hyde to take over. I call it the sin solution to duality. Of course it is not *really* a solution, but it may seem to be for a while. Sexual acting out, irresponsibility, aggressiveness, and substance abuse often result. One man said that he once gave up drinking, smoking, and chasing women all at once and that it was the worst twenty minutes of his life! Whereas the last chapter considered hiding the dark side, this chapter considers hiding everything except the dark side—a modern-day hedonism emphasizing doing whatever feels good.

Figure 6 The dark side takes over in Hiding Jekyll.

Seeking pleasure can be an addiction. Just as a drug addict seeks narcotics at any cost, those addicted to sin seek pleasure at any cost. They avoid responsibility and obscure morality in the race for fun. The dark side takes over.

But it goes beyond seeking pleasure. Imagine for a moment that a toxic substance gets into your city's water supply. The toxic chemical alters the central nervous system and everyone in the city loses control over their impulses. Everyone does just what he or she wants to do, whatever feels good. Can you imagine the implications? This theme was presented in a movie produced by ABC. A doctor choked a critically ill patient to death because he tired of her repeated incontinence; a policeman shot a young boy for opening a parking meter; citizens stole money from bank tills; and a woman repeatedly rammed another car with hers because her parking place had been taken. Impulse goes far beyond pleasure seeking and our usual ideas of impulse broaden when considering this kind of scenario. Similarly, the sin solution to duality involves more than our usual ideas of pleasure seeking, often including amazing acts of hostility and aggressiveness.

The antisocial personality disorder (a diagnosis used by mental-health professionals) illustrates an exaggerated form of the sin solution. Dark-side impulses dictate the behavior of these individuals almost exclusively. Approximately 3 percent of males and 1 percent of females in the United States have the disorder, characterized by irresponsible and impulsive behavior, lack of guilt for wrongdoing, blaming others for their own behavior, rejection of authority, and inability to maintain relationships. They frequently spend much of their lives in prison. Antisocial personality disorder is an extreme form of the sin solution. Although they seek a solution in sin and pleasure, they find no solution and very little pleasure.

The sin solution is paradoxical. What begins as a striving for pleasure often becomes a bland life of meaningless sin, a search for joy that is futile from the beginning. Actively seeking pleasure results in less pleasure than actively seeking rightness.

Assumptions

Finish this sentence, "Life should be...." I frequently prescribe this exercise to my clients. They often finish the sentence in one of two ways.

Life should be fair. Many have this assumption, probably originating early in life. Our five-year-old frequently reminds us that we are not being fair. She doesn't appreciate my reply that life isn't fair.

Psychologists call it the "just-world assumption." In one experiment a female subject was selected by lottery to receive painful electric shocks. No shocks were actually given since the real experiment was to see how onlookers responded. Consistently, onlookers responded not with sympathy but with the assumption that "she got what she deserved." We assume the world is just and fair.

The second way the above sentence is often finished is: *life should be fun.* Many assume a life without pleasure is a pointless existence. This is quite natural since the times we remember vividly are often those with great pleasure.

By putting these two assumptions together an interesting integration emerges. By combining "life should be fair" and "life should be fun," we get "it's not fair if life isn't fun." This sounds absurd at first but we often function according to this assumption. For example, "I work hard but can never save enough for that new boat or sports car. It just isn't fair." Or, "I can't spend the rest of my life with my wife because I'm in love with another woman. It just wouldn't be fair to me or my wife." The merits of fidelity are overshadowed by the one-sided presentations of free sexuality on prime-time television. Many conclude the biblical values of morality are outdated since it is difficult to live by scriptural standards and still enjoy life. So they seek pleasure without exploring the underlying assumptions. Hiding Jekyll is the result.

We can only explore these assumptions on a rational level. That life isn't fair is an existential dilemma. Carefully ponder the fate of a newborn Ethiopian child or a South African black citizen. Justice isn't a natural resource and the just-world assumption is false. In the same way, speaking of fun would seem callous to a Haitian mother whose child is slowly starving. The assumption that life should be fun is not intrinsically true. To live as if a just life is a fun life is to deny rationality and live on an impulsive level.

Development

There are several ways to explain the development of the sin solution to duality. The explanations are not mutually exclusive, making it likely that more than one have been instrumental in persons ruled by dark-side impulses.

Pseudorationality. The rational life motive seeks truth. If God is part of truth, then believing in God is rational. Ignoring God is a form of pseudorationality. Paul described this in the first chapter of Romans:

> For even though they knew God, they did not honor Him as God, or give thanks; but they became futile in their speculations, and their foolish heart was darkened. Professing to be wise, they became fools, and exchanged the glory of the incorruptible God for an image in the form of corruptible man and of birds and four-footed animals and crawling creatures (Rom. 1:21–23).

God revealed himself through creation (general revelation), so denying God disables part of our nature created in his image. Denying God is not rational, but pseudorational.

Paul addressed the result of denying the rationality of God in the same passage:

> Therefore God gave them over in the lusts of their hearts to impurity, that their bodies might be dishonored among them. For they exchanged the truth of God for a lie, and worshiped and served the creature rather than the Creator, who is blessed forever. Amen. (Rom. 1:24, 25).

This is not a lofty theological concept. It is common sense. If I, a rational being, wrongly conclude there is no God to serve, then who am I to serve? I will serve a person, a creature, rather than the God whom I believe to be nonexistent. The creature I choose to serve will probably be me. I will focus on my desires for pleasure and will pursue them. This is a spiritual explanation for hiding Jekyll.

Albert Ellis, a well-known psychologist and an outspoken atheist, once suggested that extramarital affairs can be useful and productive for some marriages. In a 1967 *New York Times* article, Ellis described the healthy adulterer as, "nondemanding and noncompulsive, but feels affirmatively that he is better off with an affair than without." Notice the focus! A healthy adulterer considers himself. He is uncomfortable with duality, as evidenced by attractions toward other women, and concludes that the best coping strategy is the sin solution. If it feels good, do it.

This is not true rationality. Neither is it rational to conclude adultery is wrong only because God said it was wrong. The consequences of adultery argue against it. Why did God prohibit adultery? What effect does adultery have on my spouse, my children, me, my new lover, my new lover's spouse and children, and so forth? These rational questions transcend Ellis's primitive reasoning that "I would be better off with an affair than without."

I don't mean to overstate this point. Most atheists live responsible lives, not exclusively characterized by sin. Sometimes their humanitarian efforts exceed those of Christians. Nonetheless, they emphasize the creature and not the Creator and serving others is seen as an end in itself rather than an extension of God's grace.

Modeling.   Life isn't fair. I was frequently left with a sense of injustice when listening to family devotions from the Old Testament as a child. I particularly remember the story of Achan. When Achan sinned by keeping treasure for himself after the destruction of

Jericho, he was destroyed along with his sons, daughters, oxen, donkeys, and sheep. They even destroyed his tent, wiping away any final trace of his existence. It just doesn't seem fair!

Children still suffer as a result of parents' sins. For example, children learn from observing parents. Parents who are indulgent, pleasure loving, and frivolous produce children who live by impulse as a way to cope with the demands of life. If parents do it because it feels good, children probably will also.

Several years ago Dan Nichols, a twenty-year-old "mountain man" was accused of kidnapping a woman and slaying her would-be rescuer. The man, according to the Associated Press article, assisted his fifty-four-year-old father in kidnapping the woman as part of a long-time plan to find a "mountain woman" for companionship. Defense attorney Steve Ungar used a novel and fascinating defense tactic. Because Nichols had been so influenced by his father, claimed the attorney, he was not able to think for himself. From a psychological perspective, this seems remotely possible. We all learn a great deal from our parents. Some of the learning is constructive and useful and some is destructive. Mr. Nichols received more than his share of destructive influence. Dark-side impulses had a strong hold on his behavior.

It still doesn't seem fair that parents' sins often cause the downfall of children. But it's true. Sin filters down through generations, creating confusion, rebellion, pain, and spiritual blindness.

Reaction to rigidity. Linda and I had been meeting for several weeks before I asked if there were significant sexual conflicts in her childhood. A soft-spoken woman in her mid-fifties, she quietly contemplated the question before saying she had hoped it would never come up in our counseling. She began describing her early childhood with some hesitation and awkwardness. I almost missed the crucial element of her revelation because I was expecting a horrific story of sexual abuse. Whenever she handled her genitals as a child, her father became outraged and told her that good girls don't do that. Her father apparently didn't know that virtually all children manipulate their genitals during preschool years, with or without their parents' permission. Linda was no exception, but because of her father's punitive reactions, she learned to be more cautious. Sexual exploration became a private "sin" for Linda. Because she was a normal child, she found pleasure in self-manipulation, all the while experiencing guilt because of her father's words. It provided immediate relief to hide her behavior, but the long-term pattern became maladaptive. Her hidden half was strengthened.

Linda's sexual behavior remained a central theme as she grew: playing doctor with children in the neighborhood, extreme promiscuity in high school and college, repeated marriages as an adult. She viewed the world in sexual terms and seemed to have little control over her sexual behavior.

Once Linda broke into tears in my office, "I don't want to be bad," she sobbed. "All I ever wanted to do was to make people happy." Linda faced an emotional dilemma. She wanted to please her father, to act like good girls act, but she was driven by the impulses of humanity in the painful grip of duality. The sin solution only made duality grow.

Here is synergism again. The glossy side evokes the dark side. Linda's home was characterized by rigid rules. She couldn't listen to radio shows because they might have a negative influence. She addressed her parents as "Ma'am" and "Sir." Anger was not allowed. The rigidity of her home did not prevent duality—it only made it private. In the fertile soil of privacy, Linda's dark side grew magnificently. It burst into prominence during teenage years and had remained in control ever since.

Again, this is paradoxical. Well-meaning parents try to protect their children from the influences of evil, but the results backfire when the expectations are excessive. Unrealistic expectations communicate to children that having a dark side is unacceptable. If it feels good, *don't* do it. When those children experience inevitable temptations, they cannot go to their parents because they fear punishment or verbal condemnation. Coping with the dark side becomes a private battle.

How many upright teenagers go off to college and get caught up in a life of overt sin? It doesn't happen suddenly. Those dark-side impulses have been growing for years but because they have not been acknowledged in the home, the child has developed no resources to manage them. College doesn't create new temptations; it only allows existing temptations to be experienced openly. The problem isn't only what happens at college; it's also what happens before college.

Results of Hiding Jekyll

Hiding Jekyll is a palliative coping strategy. It might appear useful as a relief from the struggles of duality, at least at first. But soon it becomes confusing and frustrating. As one formerly promiscuous client put it, "I've been down that road, and it's not what it seems."

Self-centeredness. Living by dark-side impulses denies the rational. Life proceeds on an impulsive, self-centered level. Gary Gilmore, who had an antisocial personality disorder, described the second of two murders for which he was executed in the following way.

> I went in and told the guy to give me the money. I told him to lay on the floor and then I shot him. I then walked out and was carrying the cash drawer with me. I took the money and threw the cash drawer in a bush and I tried to push the gun in the bush too. But as I was pushing it in the bush, it went off and that's how come I was shot in the arm. It seems like things have always gone bad for me. It seems like I've always done dumb things that just caused trouble for me.[1]

Gilmore focused on his own bad luck and concluded that things have always gone bad for him. How ironic. Immediately after taking the life of another human being, he focused on himself and had no sense of remorse for his actions.

Gilmore was an extreme. Few people are as self-centered as Gilmore, but doesn't the same logic apply when Albert Ellis concludes extramarital affairs are good for those who feel they are better off with one than without one? In both cases, the self is emphasized and the welfare of others is minimized.

1. Rosenhan, D. L., and Seligman, M. E. P. (1984). *Abnormal psychology.* New York: W. W. Norton, 440.

Self-defeating strategies. Some behaviors are self-destructive. By participating in these behaviors we defeat ourselves. Take motorcycles. One motorcyclist had an inscription on his helmet reading, **AB** NEGATIVE. I have nothing against motorcycles, but they're similar to small airplanes on my avoidance list. I like life.

The sin solution to **duality is self-defeating**. Excessive use of alcohol is a good example. People abuse alcohol to escape problems or to enjoy social occasions. Liver disease, memory deficits, loss of inhibition, and traffic deaths are just a few of the self-defeating results of alcohol. Efforts to escape problems have only created new, more serious, problems.

Bob found himself attracted to Christine, a co-worker. Falling in love is fun, and for a time Bob's anxiety was reduced after meeting Christine. He firmly believed having an affair would be morally wrong, but was unable to explore the consequences of having an affair. He could produce the glossy side (*I shouldn't have an affair*), but couldn't view the new relationship from a rational perspective (*this is* why *I shouldn't have an affair*). Bob decided to have an affair. Impulses battled and the sin solution won. His anxiety returned stronger than ever. Self-defeating behavior has emotional consequences and Bob was his own victim.

Why do we engage in self-destructive behaviors? Because we don't carefully evaluate consequences. Bob refused to view his dilemma from a rational perspective because he was so invested in the impulsive battle. The following dialogue took place inside Bob:

DARK SIDE	Go for it! It feels great to be in love.
GLOSSY SIDE	You can't have an affair, it is wrong!

DARK SIDE	Don't worry about it, just enjoy yourself.
GLOSSY SIDE	The Bible says not to commit adultery.
DARK SIDE	You can't be perfect all the time. Enjoy!
RATIONAL (*me, in this case*)	Let's consider the consequences.
DARK SIDE AND GLOSSY SIDE	Shut up and stay out of this!

The battle raged for several weeks before the dark side won. As Bob soon discovered, the sin solution is self-defeating. The glamor of sin is attractive, but its consequences are destructive.

Unsatisfactory relationships. Unable to control his impulses, Larry had sexually abused his one-year-old daughter. As a father of three young daughters, I was repulsed by Larry's behavior, making it difficult to accept Larry with a warm and caring style. I tried to deal with my feelings as I met with Larry for a period of several months.

A gay prostitute since age thirteen, Larry's life brimmed with sin. I began to realize that he was a victim of his parents' sin and soon acquired the empathy I needed as a therapist. He never had a chance! After his parents left him he shifted from foster home to foster home until he left for San Francisco at thirteen. Acting on his sexual and aggressive impulses caused him a series of problems for the years that followed. The court insisted he come to the clinic for psychological assistance.

As weeks went by, relationships came and went for Larry. There was no stability. A close friend one week was an arch enemy the next. Larry had never experienced a stable relationship. His impulsive style drove others away, and so he lived completely alone in the middle of a metropolitan area. Even abusing his daughter resulted from an unstable relationship—he reportedly did it to get back at his girlfriend! The sin solution leads to unstable relationships. Unstable relationships, in Larry's case, provoked him to greater sin.

Relationships flourish when individuals care for one another. But the sin solution focuses on self, resulting in unstable and adversarial relationships. There is great practical value in Paul's admonition:

> Do nothing from selfishness or empty conceit, but with humility of mind let each of you regard one another as more important than himself; do not merely look out for your own personal interests, but also for the interests of others (Phil. 2:3, 4).

Many cope with duality by hiding Jekyll. The appeal of sin is strong. So is the assumption that life should be fair and fun, but sin is seductive and the results are bitter. Sin is self-defeating, resulting in unstable relationships and selfcenteredness. "...the outcome of those things is death" (Rom. 6:21).

7

Answerism

> ...I sought with tears and prayers to smother down the crowd of hideous images and sounds with which my mind swarmed against me; and still, between the petitions, the ugly face of my iniquity stared into my soul. As the acuteness of this remorse began to die away, it was succeeded by a sense of joy. The problem of my conduct was solved. Hyde was thenceforth impossible; whether I would or not, I was now confined to the better part of my existence; and oh, how I rejoiced to think of it!...
>
> Dr. Jekyll

Jekyll thought he had found an answer. Since Hyde was now a murderer, he could no longer appear in public. This would provide Jekyll with motivation to suppress Hyde forever. Never again would he struggle with duality. But his efforts of suppression were destined to failure. Hyde did return despite Jekyll's sincere desire to be rid of him forever.

This is a common pattern. In the wake of sin, we feel intensely motivated to change. Zeal often causes us to share our solutions with others, implying we have found the answer to duality. But easy answers are a palliative coping strategy like hiding Hyde or hiding Jekyll. We feel better for a time but we cannot eliminate the duality fundamental to human existence. Easy answers cover up the duality only temporarily.

John came to me at the advice of his wife. A forty-five-year-old married male, he had struggled for years with his enslavement to pornography. The night before we talked his daughter had walked in on him as he was thumbing through a pornographic magazine. He was willing to do whatever it took to change. After several sessions John stopped coming for his appointments. On the phone he explained that he didn't need to see me because he had figured out his problem. By giving up television and choosing to have willpower he thought he could overcome his temptations. I hope John was right. Since I haven't seen him again, it may have worked. But I am doubtful. His efforts and motivation were appropriate but his solution was shallow, based on an impulsive answer to an impulsive problem.

Searching for Answers vs. Answerism

John's search for answers was healthy. It seems to be human instinct. We are constantly seeking answers to our problems and the problems of others. "Dear Abby," Ann Landers, Dr. Joyce Brothers, and Dr. Ruth offer solutions for personal, marital, emotional, relational, and sexual problems. Radio talk-show hosts or guests answer call-in questions.

The answer obsession has penetrated evangelicalism. The Christian self-help book market is huge—to provide answers to obesity, extramarital attractions, depression, and world hunger. A popular television evangelist has recently published a book of answers to two hundred of life's most probing questions. *Why isn't everyone healed? How do I get over depression? How do I free myself from fear? How does God guide people?* If we are not cautious, we might blindly assume easy answers exist for all these questions. We might even begin to assume there is an answer to duality.

Searching for answers is healthy. We survive by looking for new ways to cope with problems and overcome obstacles. Many times we find workable solutions to our problems because of efforts to find answers. We search for answers because we are rational beings, created in God's image.

Figure 7

Rational search for answers	**Impulsive road to answerism**
Faced with personal trial	Faced with personal trial
↓	↓
Search for answers	Search for answers
sometimes	↓
Help others in their search for answers ← *sometimes* → Find an answer	Prescribe answer to others
↓	↓
	Judge others for not agreeing or not complying
⬇	⬇
Empathy Insight Compassion	Criticalness Defensiveness Rigidity Self-justification

But the search for answers can also lead to simplistic solutions that are dispensed to others as emotional

Band-Aids. This road to "answerism" is paved with glossy-side impulses. Figure 7 illustrates the distinction between healthy searching for answers and answerism. Three differences can be noted.

Answerism always has an answer. First, those who rationally search for answers can tolerate ambiguity. They don't always find answers to the difficulties of life. In contrast, answerism always produces an answer, even if incorrect. John found an answer, but it lacked reason. Will giving up television really change the inner dynamics of personality that create his perverse desires? It might become more difficult for John to view video pornography but no inner transformation had taken place. He discovered a deterrent but not an answer.

Sometimes we may be guilty of answerism when we evangelize. It seems natural that becoming a Christian will solve problems. Certainly becoming a Christian does solve many problems, including the crucial problem of eternal damnation, but duality persists even after discovering the power of Christ. Someone recently brought a tract to our home implying Christianity resolves all life conflicts. By saying a prayer the reader could be freed from drugs, alcohol, marital problems, depression, hopelessness, loneliness, frustration, or suicidal feelings. Is it really that easy? The power of God is limitless but he chooses to allow us to continue our battle with duality, even after conversion.

Figure 8 illustrates our traditional approach to viewing life. Questions linger on the surface, but for each question there exists a specific answer. It's like eighth-grade algebra. Problems appearing to have no solution seem simple when the teacher scribbles the solution on the chalkboard. Similarly, we perceive all other problems in life to have an answer. We go to the pastor with questions about spiritual maturity, to the attorney with questions about legal conflicts, to the physician with health questions, and to the psychologist with questions about emotional disturbance or marital adjustment. In each case we expect a quick or final answer. When the physician looks the patient in the eye and says, "I'm sorry but it is a terminal disease," the patient suddenly is confronted with a void. Seeing no apparent answer to the ultimately painful problem of death, the patient looks frantically for another explanation. Second opinions and miracle cures are pursued; still no answers are found.

**Figure 8 Traditional view: answers underlie
the significant questions of life.**

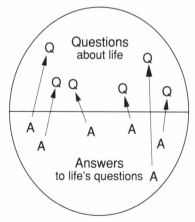

I recently spent an entire psychotherapy session trying to convince a client I could not help her reach her goal of completely eliminating the temptation to abuse alcohol. "Although it may be somewhat reduced with counseling, that temptation will continue for years," I said, "and the only thing that can be controlled is your response to the temptation." She left with dashed hopes because she so wanted to eliminate the temptation. How can one get rid of temptations that have existed for years? She was looking for an answer that I didn't have. Insisting that answers always exist is what the glossy side would have us do, but it simply isn't true.

Figure 9 represents a more accurate view. That some questions in life have concrete answers cannot be denied. Answers can be found for questions about how to install a garbage disposal, or how to drive a car with a manual transmission. But beyond answers like these lies a more fundamental level of questions. These are deep questions for which we have no final answers. They might be called existential questions because they are basic to human existence. What does it mean to die? Is it acceptable to take the life of another human? Who is God? Why does a merciful God allow suffering? How can I cope with my dual nature? Although rational contemplation of these existential questions is important, we will never arrive at answers totally resolving the questions. We might be able to answer some questions to our own satisfaction, but our answers will not completely resolve the inherent mystery of the questions. Interestingly, God never attempted to answer the profound questions raised by Job in the midst of his suffering. God knows best that answers to such questions defy human understanding.

Figure 9 **Alternative view: Answers underlie some questions in life, but a deeper level of existential questions exists which defies human answers.**

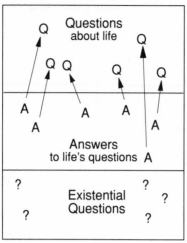

Answerism prescribes answers to others. Those searching rationally for answers are less inclined to insist others agree with their answers. Many times I've encountered anger in response to the phrase, "God causes these things to work for his good" (*see* Rom. 8:28). A woman whose husband left her for another woman heard this verse as consolation from well-meaning Christian friends. She hid her anger under a polite nod. Although God causes us to mature as we experience pain, in the midst of pain an answer is often the last thing we want to hear. When a loved one dies, we struggle with deep questions about the meaning of death and the nature of existence. Christian platitudes seem trite and meaningless because they imply easy answers to the questions that torment us. Even true answers are sometimes not appropriate to prescribe for others.

Such answers can come from worthy motives but often are knee-jerk reflexes to trials. "If you have marital problems, the wife needs to submit more and try praying together." "If you are depressed, you need more Christian fellowship and prayer." "If you have problems with a recurrent sin, you need Bible study and true repentance." These answers are not wrong necessarily, but they are often reflexive, reflecting little evaluation or rationality.

Answerism judges others for noncompliance.   Several years ago Christian sociologist Tony Campolo spoke in the chapel at the college where I teach. He compared the motives of power and love. Power seeks to raise oneself whereas love seeks to help another. The distinction between answerism and a healthy search for answers is similar. Answerism seeks power by insisting others comply with the answers given, whereas the healthy quest for answers seeks truth.

A fitting analogy is the biblical admonition not to judge others (Matt. 7:1–5). Does this mean we have to abandon church discipline? Of course not. Matthew records Jesus' recommendations for church discipline later in his Gospel (Matt. 18). The difference between judging and discipline is a matter of motives. Pharisees loved to judge because it elevated their religious stance. True discipline involves a painful search for truth. Judging is self-centered whereas biblical discipline is truth-centered.

Similarly, answers are appropriate when they aren't judgmental and self-serving. If you give me directions when I stop in your town, you are serving me and not yourself. If I advise a client to avoid an extramarital affair, I am serving my client and not myself. These answers are rational, considering truth more than self. Other answers tend to exalt oneself over another. If I tell a client struggling with duality to study the Bible and to pray every day for a week and the temptations will go away, I might be (but not necessarily) exalting myself by implying I have risen above such temptation.

This distinction comes down to motives and not content. If I see someone in need and tell him or her that God causes all things to work together for good, it might have varying effects. If it is done out of genuine concern and compassion, the other person will sense empathy and receive the comment with benefit. If, however, the comment comes as a Band-Aid answer, the receiving party will sense the lack of genuine concern. The content of the message was the same in either case but the motives differed. In the first case the motive was genuine concern rather than self-serving answerism. It is the difference between the rationality made in God's image and the glossy side that seeks power and to please self.

James distinguishes between true wisdom and selfish wisdom in James 3:13–18. Selfish wisdom is evidenced by jealousy, disorder, and evil. It is a pseudo-wisdom, a pretend rationality. In contrast, pure wisdom is peaceable, gentle, reasonable, and full of mercy. These characteristics of pure wisdom might be a good way to evaluate motives when giving answers.

Answerism is very different from a healthy search for answers. It always has an answer, it prescribes answers to others, and it judges others for noncompliance. Answerism is the result of power and not love.

Glossy Side Disguised

The glossy side seeks easy answers. It starts as a personal process. Assuming that answers always exist, the glossy side finds an answer to every problem. But answerism grows and soon involves others. The glossy side soon starts insisting that others seek the same answers and come to the same conclusions. Wearing the cloak of rationality, the glossy side gives well-timed answers appearing to reflect profound thought. If I can provide an answer for your question, I could appear to be spiritually wise and mature. It could be a self-serving strategy that builds me up as I subtly put you down. I could be asserting that if you were only as spiritual as I, then you would have thought of the answer yourself.

Ordering my first computer almost discouraged me enough to keep me from personal computers forever. I called the manufacturer every few days for more than a month. At first they told me they had to make one final change in the operating system but assured me it would be in the mail within a few days. Next they told me the computer was ready, but there had been too many requests. Finally they told me one had been shipped and would be arriving within a week. Days passed, and the computer didn't come. I called again, and they said they would send it out the next day. The reality of their tactics became clear several weeks later when the computer arrived, and it didn't work. Not wanting their customers to lose confidence, they had been creating stories to explain the delays being caused by problems

with their product. All of their excuses seemed
rational, but they were self-serving. They had been
focusing on the appearance of their company, disguising self-serving answers with supposedly rational explanations. I didn't buy the computer.

In Christianity we sometimes disguise the glossy
side in rationality and resort to answerism. Three of the
common disguises are:

The Bible says.... Perhaps the most common
form of answerism in Christianity is the arbitrary use
of Scripture. The Bible says_____ therefore the answer is _____. At first this may sound heretical, but
give me a chance to explain. I believe in the Bible as the
authoritative, inspired word of God.

**Figure 10 Answerism is the disguising of glossy-side
impulses with apparent rationality. Dark-side
impulses are often hidden, even from oneself.**

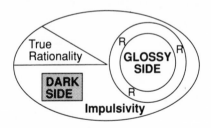

What the Bible supposedly endorses is amazing. One
gentleman showed me where the Bible said honey is
healthy and thus concluded that sugar is not (*see* Prov.
24:13). I later consulted with a colleague who assured
me honey is just like other forms of sugar except it is
dirtier, since the bees have been walking through it! In
some geographical areas, people present biblical evi-

dence that the King James Version is the only acceptable translation. Others claim the Bible says it's against
nature or against God's will for a black person to marry
a Caucasian. In the mid-nineteenth century, politicians
and preachers used the Bible to support slavery in
America. Centuries earlier, the Bible "affirmed" that
the earth is flat. The Bible has been and still is used
arbitrarily to support conclusions that are not really
scriptural.

Obviously the answer is to interpret Scripture correctly. Accurate interpretation involves rational understanding. If the Bible is understood rationally, then it is
less likely to be used in a self-serving way to support
one's prior conclusions. Using our intellect to study
God's Word is appropriate. Although we need theo-
logians and pastors, accepting something as true just
because we are told that by spiritual leaders can lead us
into the confusion of answerism.

Some conclude that since human logic is insufficient
to understand God's purposes, we should focus only on
obedience rather than understanding. If this were true,
why did God give us a rational nature at all? Animals
can learn to obey. Only humans can understand.
Nietzsche's words, "He who has a why to live can bear
almost any how," apply well. Rules backed by good
reasons can be tolerated. Arbitrary rules, however,
evoke dark-side rebellion. It is the difference between
rational rules and glossy-side rules.

Of course, at times we choose—or have no choice
but—to obey without fully understanding God's inten-
tion. But even this obedience is rational if we view faith
as rational. By faith we believe that following God's

Word will be productive and will honor him. Our faith is, in turn, based on objective, positive experiences with God and his people and is therefore rationally founded.

If Scripture is interpreted correctly, we will usually understand the *whys*. If we don't steal only because the Bible says not to, we are missing out on much of the value of rationality. The consequences of stealing are social chaos and great insensitivity to others. There are good reasons for the command not to steal.

The Pharisees believed in answerism. They knew the law forward, backward, and sideways. Alleged rationality was their disguise, but they weren't really very rational. They applied the law when Jesus wanted to heal a man's withered hand (*see* Mark 3). The Pharisees had the answer. Jesus could have walked away from that man in need. But Jesus functioned on the rational level. He understood the purpose of the law and knew that to walk away would be evil rather than good (v. 4). Jesus understood the *why* behind the law and he acted accordingly.

Pulling a single Bible verse out of context and announcing, "The Bible says..." can be a form of answerism. The broader context of Scripture and God's love need to be considered so rationalism can extend into our use of God's Word.

Christian paranoia. Another common disguise for answerism is found in the reaction to secular ideas. The church hierarchy has been repeatedly opposed to scientific advances throughout history. A round earth, a sun-centered solar system, and the treatment of mental illness are a few examples. When the evidence became so overwhelmingly strong that it could not be denied, the church officials backed off and admitted the veracity of scientific findings. Often doctrinal inter- pretation is changed to accommodate new scientific understanding. Are our answers truly rational or are they defensive? Could they reflect a fear of change? The current critique of "secular humanism" provides a use- ful example.

While the dangers of secular expressions of human- ism are real, Christians have often overreacted by misrepresenting humanism. Humanists have been identified in Christian literature as monolithic and as promoters of pornography, marijuana, drugs, self- indulgence, rights without responsibilities, and disillu- sionment with America. Humanists are no more in- clined to accept these labels than Christians would be. Such one-sided presentations of humanism create a straw man wearing a black hat at which Christians can throw spiritual darts. David Bollier described this as a "witch hunt" against secular humanism. A victim of the witch hunt, Christian sociologist Tony Campolo was recently canceled from an evangelical program because his faith was perceived as prostituted to secu- lar humanism. In a cartoon reprinted in *Christianity Today* (9/27/85), Campolo holds a white vial labeled BIBLE TRUTH in one hand and a black vial labeled HU- MANISM (beneath a skull and crossbones) in the other. The caricature was unfortunate because Christians can learn from sensitive scholars like Campolo, especially if we are tolerant of minor doctrinal differences.

Is humanism as such really the enemy? Historically, humanism has been an integral part of Christianity since the Renaissance because of the emphasis on concern for those less fortunate. Humanists have been passionately invested in social justice. Clearly Christianity and humanism are not mutually exclusive. One can be both a Christian and a humanist. Many of the emphases are very similar. For example, both emphasize social compassion for others in need, the merit of personal growth and responsibility, the value of suffering, the distinction between animal and human, and the place for proactive decision making.

Extreme reactions to humanism might have some rational basis, but might also be fueled by a form of Christian paranoia that has reacted to secularism in many forms for centuries. If it is the latter, we need to be cautious not to be involved in mindless answerism.

Asceticism revisited. When Paul wrote his epistle to the church at Colossae, they were struggling with the heresy of asceticism—the belief that the body was inherently evil, emphasizing self-righteousness through self-sacrifice.

> If you have died with Christ to the elementary principles of the world, why, as if you were living in the world, do you submit yourself to decrees, such as, "Do not handle, do not taste, do not touch!" (which all refer to things destined to perish with the using)—in accordance with the commandments and teachings of men? These are matters which have, to be sure, the appearance of wisdom in self-made religion and self-abasement and severe treatment of the body, but are of no value against fleshly indulgence (Col. 2:20–23).

Paul then called his readers to seek the things above, setting their minds on Christ. The difference is apparent. With asceticism, the mind is set on self. "This is what I must do to be deserving of salvation." It's a doctrine not only of works, but also a doctrine of merit. "How can I be good enough to deserve God's salvation of grace?" The mind is set on self.

Paul advocated that we set our minds on Christ. Rather than excessive concern about ourselves and our worthiness, we are to focus on Christ. How can I understand the grace of God through Jesus Christ? This is one of those deep questions. As we ponder that profound question, we become overwhelmed in his beauty and not in our unworthiness.

Modern-day answerism often comes in a plethora of rules. This is not surprising when one considers how convenient rules are. Rules provide a sanitized system for determining or controlling behavior. Rather than thinking, we can consult our list of rules. Our children have learned not to touch merchandise while we're shopping. They do not understand why, but they obey because it is a rule. Later on they will know the reasons behind the rule. Lisa and I, for now, are comfortable with the rule because it makes shopping with our small children much less of a hassle. Rules work efficiently.

At the Christian college where I teach, many rules exist for appropriate conduct. While I'm glad we have the rules to preserve the distinctively Christian nature of the college, I am constantly aware of the dangers of asceticism. Students might begin to base their spirituality upon their adherence to the rules. Higher morality extends beyond rules. Jesus defied some traditional rules in his earthly demonstration of truth. He independently evaluated popularly held dogmas and traditions.

Asceticism is a form of answerism. It seeks to diminish the wonder of God's grace with self-sacrifice. If I give up all enjoyable things in my life, then I feel more worthy of God's love. Asceticism reflects the glossy side because it focuses on self.

Righteousness or Self-Righteousness?

Asceticism, seeking an easy answer to God's grace by emphasizing self-sacrifice, might be more prevalent in Christianity than we know. Consider two of the activities that we value in evangelical Christianity: witnessing and personal devotions.

Witnessing. Guilt about not witnessing is a common spiritual defeat I see in working with clients. This leads me to wonder whether some believers witness to non-Christians primarily to reduce guilt. They become indignant when non-Christians talk of the lunatic evangelicals out to get notches on their belts. "Our motives are misunderstood," they say. Perhaps non-Christians are more perceptive than we acknowledge.

Note the difference between a salesperson who sells just to make a good living and a salesperson who believes the product will sell itself. If the product will sell itself, the salesperson does no more than demonstrate the product and leaves the decision to the customer. If, however, the salesperson is more concerned with making a living, all kinds of tactics are used to keep the customer in the store. A customer leaving with a sigh of relief signifies disdain for the high-pressure sales approach.

Do we believe God's grace sells itself? If so, our task is to introduce others to the joy and meaning that a rational understanding of God can bring. We can be vocal at this task—certainly the New Testament evangelists were—but sales pressure is unnecessary. Our New Testament exemplars allowed their listeners to make their own decisions without coercion. When I hear non-Christians complaining about overzealous evangelicals, it's usually because of sales pressure. Can we just dismiss their objections as misguided? Perhaps high-pressure sales tactics reflect a self-serving need for answerism and guilt reduction at least as often as a sincere desire to introduce others to God's grace.

Personal devotions.   Some denominations emphasize quiet times (or personal devotions) more than others. Again it is important to look for motivation. Personal devotions in response to the wonder of God's grace are very different than personal devotions out of asceticism, as a mechanism to reduce guilt.

Some Christians claim that a day without devotions is like a day without sunshine or a morning without orange juice. Where is the emphasis? If I am having devotions so my day will go well, am I focusing mostly on myself? It might be a form of answerism to deal with the problems of the day.

Devotions have been the richest for me during the times I felt no obligation. When I respond to God's love voluntarily by reading his Word or sitting in quiet meditation, his goodness often overwhelms me. It is not uncommon for tears to well in my eyes and, for a few moments, to gain a greater understanding of God, his love, his mercy, and his grace. Could it be that this is what Paul meant when he instructed the Colossians to set their minds on things above?

Results of Answerism

As with the other palliative coping strategies for duality, answerism has adverse side-effects. Why do churches split? I won't give an easy answer to that question, to be consistent, but it might be related to the results of answerism.

Criticalness. Lay leadership was a distinctive of one church group with which Lisa and I were happily involved for several years. Rather than having a pastor, various individuals in the congregation would preach at Sunday-morning services. It was a nice church government system that came closer to the New Testament model than most, but the preaching services were sometimes unpredictable. One Sunday speaker was a towering man with excellent knowledge of the Bible, but he communicated poorly. I sat during one service trying to listen to him intently. Since I was scheduled to speak the following week, I found myself noticing the psychology of the congregation instead. Old men slept, children whispered, and many sat staring blandly into space. Few were listening. The following Sunday, I made a special effort to gain attention by using humor and illustrations to help the congregation listen. I discussed unity in the church, using Philippians 2.

People seemed especially pleased. Elders informed me of the appropriateness of the message since some disunity was occurring without my awareness. Suddenly, the man who spoke the previous week was extending his hand. We had never met formally before so he introduced himself. Without a smile he handed me a note card and asked me to call him that afternoon. I curiously looked at the note card:

Mark McMinn:

Why do you think you can render Philippians 2:2 as "interest?" What are your thoughts that enable you to render the 4 conditional clauses of vs. 1 into "commit?"

He was more of a biblical scholar than I. On the phone that afternoon I mentioned the sources I had used to interpret the passage. I used his valid criticisms as I prepared other messages, but more than correct interpretation was at issue. Ironically, a message on unity evoked a response of answerism. In gradually piecing together that experience, I derived an explanation (my explanation might be biased since I was disturbed by his behavior). He was threatened by my style. He viewed the pulpit as a place for bland teaching, not a place for humor. Criticism served as a defense to "put me in my place." It was a form of answerism.

Defensiveness.   Answerism doesn't stop with correct interpretation of biblical passages. It extends into the range of deep questions that defy human understanding. As such, answerism seeks to resolve the dilemma of duality. A weapon in the battle to conquer duality is the defense of denial.

Denial is to convince oneself that an aspect of reality does not exist. Answerism denies the dark-side impulses. In hiding Hyde, the dark side is hidden from others. In answerism, the dark side is often hidden even from oneself. The progression makes sense. First, I might tell myself and others that there is an answer to duality, that more time in personal devotions is needed, for example. Then, when dark-side impulses come, I either need to find a way to deny those impulses or else admit that my answer to duality does not work. Denial is often selected.

Denial of emotion can produce a nasty side-effect: physical illness. One woman I counseled for many months had fourteen major surgeries before the age of fifty. She denied most of her emotions. According to her, she never got angry, never felt sorry for herself, or never felt lonely. As we worked on her emotional understanding, her physical problems improved. Unfortunately, when she stopped coming to the psychology clinic her denial revived, and she was readmitted for her fifteenth major surgery several weeks later.

We often try to smother our anger with euphemisms. "I'm not angry, I'm hurt." "I'm not angry, I'm indignant." The effect is denial.

Rigidity. A cartoon in a Christian magazine showed a teacher drawing an evolution chart on the board of her biology classroom as she says, "Darwin said it, I believe it, and that settles it for me." We are amused at the rigidity of the evolutionist's perspective. But hold on! That cartoon caption is a parody of us. Christians used this line first. "God said it, I believe it, and that settles it for me."

If God really said it, and is the author of all truth, then we need not fear evaluation. Let's be open-minded and encourage careful evaluation of what we believe. If our foundation for believing is firm, then nothing can crumble with investigation.

A basketball coach told Tommy to guard number 22, "Stay on him wherever he goes." Several minutes later he noticed that only four players were on the court. Sure enough, there was Tommy standing in front of the crowd, guarding number 22 who was now sitting on the bench. There are similar risks for us as Christians. To get our instructions and then to follow them mindlessly is dangerous. Let's constantly investigate our convictions and hold up our beliefs for scrutiny.

Christians have had many cultural or ethnic traditions, condemning alcohol, tobacco, social dancing, movies, and playing cards. Which of these beliefs are essential to evangelical Christianity? I don't have a full answer, but I believe careful evaluation is a better alternative than adhering to traditional dogma. If a doctrine is true, then it can be supported in God's image with rationality. Jesus was not satisfied with the traditional answers of the Jewish leaders. He subjected his beliefs to rational, truth-centered analyses and sometimes came to conclusions that offended the Jewish leaders.

For example, I practice total abstinence from alcohol but not because of religious tradition or Scriptural passages. In fact, biblical evidence for total abstinence is very hard to find. So my decision to abstain comes more from personal evaluation than from Christian dogma. First, I simply don't like the taste of alcohol. Second, I object to financially supporting an industry that perpetuates unnecessary death, illness, and family crises. Other Christians have constructed rational arguments for drinking alcohol in moderation. My point is that we do best to *think* openly about issues rather than blindly accept traditional dogma as truth.

Self-justification. A substantial body of social-psychological research suggests our behavior often determines our attitudes. This seems contrary to common sense. We typically think we behave according to our attitudes. More accurately, we appear to form attitudes by observing our behavior.

This is implicitly dangerous in answerism. We might tend to disguise our impulses by finding attitudes to explain our behavior, thus denying that they are really impulses. Some Christian parents who physically abuse their children have a proverb to support this practice. "Spare the rod, spoil the child." But what if their behaviors are determining their attitudes rather than vice versa? If parents punish children out of their own aggressive impulses spawned in moments of frustration, they can later justify themselves by teaching others that physical punishment is good for children. Their behavior has determined their attitude. They now have an easy answer for parenting: physical punishment.

One woman did not let Christians in her home because she was physically abused as a child in the name of God. She wanted nothing to do with a God like that.

I'm not opposed to physical punishment categorically, but other forms of discipline can be used without "sparing the rod" completely. Physical punishment is not the single answer to good parenting. It is only one tool that's too easily overused. To advocate it as the main method of good parenting may be answerism stemming from self-justification.

As a palliative coping strategy, answerism provides immediate relief from duality by suggesting answers will lead to escape. But it focuses on self in a form of modern asceticism. Truth is obscured and self is magnified through criticism, rigidity, defensiveness, and self-justification. Apart from the wonder of God and his grace, there are no final answers to some of the dilemmas of life, including duality.

8

Meism

> ... That part of me which I had the power of
> projecting, had lately been much exercised and
> nourished; it had seemed to me of late as though
> the body of Edward Hyde had grown in stature, as
> though (when I wore that form) I were conscious
> of a more generous tide of blood; and I began to
> spy a danger that, if this were much prolonged,
> the balance of my nature might be permanently
> overthrown, the power of voluntary change be
> forfeited, and the character of Edward Hyde
> become irrevocably mine....
>
> Dr. Jekyll

I was recently watching a television rerun of "Little
House on the Prairie" in which the local merchant's
son decided to marry rather than go to college as his
mother wanted. Looking compassionately at his son as
the background music caressed viewers' emotions, the
merchant said, "If it feels right to you, then it's right." I
was shocked! This wholesome family television program had defined morality in a mindlessly limited way.
If it feels right, then it's right. What about the broader
concepts of responsibility and welfare of the com-
munity?

Television isn't the villain because it just reflects the values of society. The local merchant was telling his son, and much of America, what society wants to hear. We value individuality, independence, original thinking, and personal satisfaction. In a society with these values, Mr. Hyde seduces many into a life of meism. As answerism makes the glossy side appear rational, meism makes the dark side appear rational and natural.

Figure 11 Meism is the disguising of dark-side impulses with apparent rationality.

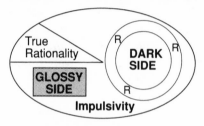

Palliative coping strategies, including meism, remove the conflicts of duality for a season. Meism ignores rationality in moral decision making and leads to the same self-defeating patterns as the other palliative coping strategies—hiding Hyde, hiding Jekyll, and answerism.

Hedonism, Meism, and Hiding Jekyll

Seeking pleasure comes so naturally that ethical theories of hedonism are almost as ancient as human nature. Hedonists see pleasure as good, pain as something to avoid, and happiness as the ultimate goal. In egoistic hedonism each individual pursues his or her own pleasure. Some philosophers advocated doing this by seeking pleasurable sensations. Eat, drink, and be merry was the philosophy of Aristippus of Cyrene about 400 B.C. Other philosophers, such as Epicurus, advocated avoiding mental pain and seeking serenity. Clearly, some forms of egoistic hedonism are opposed to altruism. Helping others or giving money to the poor might be avoided by many hedonists because it lessens one's own resources for pleasure. I need to be careful not to paint an overly critical picture of any philosophy, even hedonism. Epicurus, for example, has often been misrepresented. But any form of egoistic hedonism is best viewed skeptically by thinking Christians.

Social hedonists have a broader perspective. Also called utilitarianism, social hedonism attempts to promote good over evil, pleasure over pain for the greatest number. Giving money to the poor would be very appropriate in social hedonism if it causes the greatest number to experience pleasure.

Distinguishing between egoistic and social hedonism is important because there is a related distinction between hiding Jekyll and meism. Both hiding Jekyll and meism are hedonistic. Both seek pleasure, but use different world views. Hiding Jekyll is a willful abandoning of morality resulting in egoistic hedonism. Because rules are oppressive, egoistic hedonists decide, like Aristippus, that the temporal pleasures are more important than adhering to a list of rules. We've all heard the claim, "I want to go to hell because that's where all my friends will be." This is the essence of hiding Jekyll.

Social hedonism is more viable as a philosophical system. We lock up criminals to do good for the greatest number of people. Because we value convenience and productivity, we increase speed limits to sixty-five, knowing that more lives will be lost. Social hedonism seeks the greatest good for the greatest number. Utilitarianism is a reasonable ethical system that can't be dismissed as a primitive way of ethical reasoning. Many brilliant philosophers adhere to utilitarianism. It is reasonable hedonism.

Meism, like utilitarianism, is hedonism covered with reason. Meism differs in that it doesn't focus specifically on the greatest good for the greatest number. Instead, meists reason that the greatest number will be happy if everyone looks out for him or herself. Many humanistic philosophers and psychologists have championed this perspective. The goal of meism is not selfish but quite noble. Human potential will be reached, according to meism, only as individuals strive to meet their own potentials.

Despite the noble intentions, notice that meism results in the same shallow view of truth as egoistic hedonism. Truth, to the meist, is whatever leads to pleasure and prevents pain. When stripped of the broader social interest of utilitarianism, meists emphasize personal feelings in determining truth. "If it feels right to you, then it's right." Meism limits truth. Truth is much bigger than personal feelings or meeting one's potential.

The Big Picture

It wouldn't have been necessary to debate whether the world is flat or round if astronauts were around in the 1400s. Astronauts see the "big picture" from the camera eyes of their space ships. Similarly, rational understanding can help us see the "big picture."

But meism obscures true rationality. Meism results in a little picture, a limited view of one's own world. Propositional truth and history are overlooked. I read of a thirty-year-old actor with AIDS. After admitting he contracted AIDS through sexual contact with another man, he said, "I don't believe that AIDS is something to be ashamed of, something that I should have to keep a secret. I am very proud of who I am, very proud of the things I'm trying to do." This is a nice little picture. In the midst of a crisis, he is able to maintain a sense of self-worth and is proud of what he is doing. But the picture is bigger than what he sees. One study indicated that half of homosexual males have had more than five hundred different sexual partners.[1] It's not surprising that AIDS is epidemic. I'm not trying to make a moralistic statement, but to point out the impending social consequences of *promiscuous* homosexuality in our society. If the problem with AIDS is to be lessened, homosexuals will need to see beyond meism, beyond being proud of who they are and what they're trying to do, and see the bigger picture of the destructive nature of promiscuous behavior. Utilitarianists view the broader social consequences whereas meists naively assume social welfare will be most enhanced by "doing your own thing."

My point is not to argue the merits of utilitarianism. My intent is to demonstrate that truth-seeking goes beyond doing what *feels* right. Rationality seeks truth, even if personally inconvenient. Meism avoids truth

1. Meredith, N. (1984). The gay dilemma. *Psychology today*, 1, 56–62.

leading to self-sacrifice. My children talk of Ethiopia frequently. They seem to be so aware of the pain and suffering going on in Third World countries. I think of those unfortunate situations sometimes, but too often I'm absorbed in a new writing project or a new course preparation, or refinishing the dining-room furniture. Of course it would be of no use to sit around and worry about Ethiopia all day, but I wonder if in my preoccupations with a busy life, I sometimes miss the bigger picture. I'm living in a society where meism is accepted, and it's easy to be seduced into seeing the little picture.

Strolling along the Oregon coast allows me to escape. Majestic waves tower over a desolate beach where thoughts flow freely. I meet with God during these times when I escape the hassles of daily obligations and transcend my little picture. During these times I grow in understanding the value of grace, hope, and pain; concepts that will be discussed in subsequent chapters. Abraham Maslow wrote of "peak experiences," times when we can understand more reality than usual. I have to remove myself from daily pressures to see the bigger picture. Transcending my limited picture is a peak experience.

Happiness

Happiness is a fundamental goal of hedonism. R.G. Ingersoll, who said help for the living is the only religion, also said that happiness is the only good. The pursuit of happiness seems to be one of our inalienable rights as Americans. But we overrate happiness. How many times have you heard the phrase "She's happy and that's all that really matters." Is happiness really all that matters?

From a Roman jail Paul told the church at Philippi to rejoice in the Lord always. Paul must have been experiencing joy but Paul wasn't having fun sitting in a dank prison cell anticipating death. Maybe it depends on how we pursue happiness. Paul was joyful because of the true meaning in his life, but he was not happy in a hedonistic sense.

When happiness is pursued through love, wealth, fame, or immediate pleasures it is elusive. In *Revolt of Islam*, Shelley wrote:

> Ye seek for happiness—alas, the day!
> Ye find it not in luxury nor in gold,
> Nor in the fame, nor in the envied sway
> For which, O willing slaves to Customs old,
> Severe taskmistress! ye your hearts have sold.

Paul found joy in looking for God's meaning in the midst of his suffering. He searched for truth rather than happiness. But the message of meism is that we deserve to be happy. It's not fair if life isn't fun.

Pursuing happiness may lead to short-term satisfaction, but it is a palliative coping strategy. We become what Jackson Browne called "happy idiots," except that we often aren't very happy. But Paul's pursuit of truth led to a transcendent joy and hope that cannot be explained in human terms. Pursuing truth is different from pursuing happiness. The pursuit of truth will be considered more in the next chapter.

You're Worth It

Remember the commercial where the beautiful model finishes the cosmetic pitch with a seductive smile and the well-devised phrase, "It costs a little more, but I'm worth it"? What are we really worth? This question can be answered from many different perspectives. Biologists occasionally remind us that we are worth $1.49 in chemicals, or is it $2.49 with inflation? Or much, much more? Models inform us that our $1.49 body is worth $10.00 mascara. Some television evangelists tell us we are worth nothing apart from God. Others say that we are infinitely worthwhile because we are created in God's image.

It's difficult to appraise worth. Worth depends on underlying assumptions. Senators have different assumptions than their constituents when they vote themselves pay raises. We see ourselves as special, unique individuals and put a high price tag on ourselves. Usually that price tag is excessively high. For example, people rate themselves above average in most traits. Most people rated themselves more intelligent than average in a large *Psychology Today*[2] survey. Respondents rated themselves above average in leadership ability, athletic ability, and social skills in other surveys. We see ourselves as special and unique.

Meism builds seemingly rational arguments to support the egocentrism of the dark side. "You only live once, so you might as well enjoy it." "If you don't look out for yourself, no one else will." "It's your destiny."

2. Berscheid, E., Walster, E., and Bohrnstedt, G. (Nov. 1973). The happy American body: A survey report. *Psychology today*, 119–123, 126–131.

"You have to do what feels right for you." The messages of meism are saturated with reason. But contrast these messages with Paul's admonitions:

> Be devoted to one another in brotherly love; give preference to one another in honor;...Be of the same mind toward one another; do not be haughty in mind, but associate with the lowly. Do not be wise in your own estimation (Rom. 12:10, 16).

> Do nothing from selfishness or empty conceit, but with humility of mind let each of you regard one another as more important than himself; do not merely look out for your own personal interests, but also for the interests of others (Phil. 2:3–4).

> Therefore consider the members of your earthly body as dead to immorality, impurity, passion, evil desire, and greed, which amounts to idolatry.... Do not lie to one another, since you laid aside the old self...and have put on the new self who is being renewed to a true knowledge according to the image of the One who created him (Col. 3:5, 9, 10).

Paul considers us new creatures with a bigger picture than meism. We begin to see new significance in God's creation and to look beyond what we deserve, seeing what is true; seeing our worth through God's eyes rather than the eyes of a meistic society.

Me-nothing-ism

Karen was drowning in self-pity. She called long-distance to my home almost every night to tell me she was suicidal. Each night I talked with her about her feelings of worthlessness. But after a while I tired of her frequent calls. I soon realized that she used her worthlessness as a strategy. She wanted me to tell her how worthwhile she really was, to hear of her worth. It became a game. Karen moaned of her worthlessness, expecting her caring listener to affirm her value. I caught on after many calls and told Karen I wouldn't talk with her about suicide. She stopped calling and became less depressed. Without the payoff, her self-worth game lost meaning.

This is not a common pattern and most suicide threats *should* be taken seriously. Karen's was a special situation. Her self-esteem wasn't as poor as it appeared. Hers was a different form of meism. Karen continued her game with others as we met in counseling for the next year. Not surprisingly, she drove others away. They were understanding and sympathetic at first, but soon tired of her unceasing demands for attention. Their rejection added evidence supporting Karen's conclusion that she was worthless.

The Pharisees also used me-nothing-ism. They looked miserable when they fasted, wanting others to notice their piety. Underneath their disguises, they searched for approval from others. Neither Karen nor the Pharisees could understand the depth of Jesus' love. Karen insisted, with a slight grin on her face, that she was not worth God's love. The Pharisees thought the love of Jesus too easy; he didn't have enough rules associated with his love.

Here is another paradox. Meism and me-nothing-ism appear as opposites but are actually very similar. Both attempt self-affirmation, both obscure the "bigger picture" of God's truth, and both lead to absorption in oneself.

Self-Esteem vs. Self-Glorification

For the past fifty years psychologists have been interested in "self." Carl Jung, Alfred Adler, Erich Fromm, Abraham Maslow, Gordon Allport, Carl Rogers, and many others wrote about self-esteem, self-image, self-realization, and self-actualization. They have many useful perspectives on the importance of accurate self-esteem. However, some writers have confused these ideas and seem to emphasize self to the exclusion of concern for others. Book titles such as *Looking Out for Number One* and *Pulling Your Own Strings* make this danger clear. Self-esteem, self-glorification, and meism have become jumbled as the dark side has been cloaked in the thin rationality of psychological jargon. But this isn't true psychology.

Classic "self" psychologists clearly distinguished self-esteem from the self-love of meism. Selfishness is not part of the psychologically mature individual, according to Allport. Fromm, Adler, Maslow, Allport, and Rogers all emphasized that a healthy self-esteem results in reaching beyond oneself and becoming invested in the concerns of others. Those with healthy self-esteems are rarely selfish.

Consider a marksman shooting at a target. The marksman is more concerned with accuracy than with whether the shot is low or high. A marksman would never conclude "the higher the better." Similarly psychologists are interested in accuracy of self-concept. It may be important to observe whether self-esteem is low or high, but only so it can be adjusted accurately. Very few psychologists conclude "the higher the better." The goal is not meism or self-glorification.

Paul told his readers to think accurately about themselves, with sound judgment, rather than thinking more highly than was accurate (Rom. 12:3). Accuracy of self-esteem is different than exaltation of self. With Christian maturity we focus our attentions more and more upon God's character. Meism makes this impossible, because self absorbs all attention. Me-nothing-ism is similar because self again receives all the attention.

Results of Meism

Self-justification. Self-justification was discussed in the last chapter. After observing our behaviors we create an attitude to justify it. Meism carries with it the danger of self-justification.

I recently noticed a full-page newspaper advertisement with the challenge "Do YOU Have the Courage to Be Rich?" Americans value prosperity. The prosperity model has taken hold of American religion with significant influence. A well-known evangelist has titled her recent book *How to Have More in a Have Not World*.

Christians aren't always called to be poor, but Jesus said the love of money is a hindrance in seeking the kingdom of God. He sent away the rich young ruler because he was not willing to part with his money.

Self-justification of wealth is not surprising in our affluent society. Many adjust their attitudes to make their behavior acceptable. Some glamorize financial prosperity, making it a spiritual virtue.

Before those of us who are not wealthy feel too smug, we should remember the self-justification of answerism. We may not justify our wealth, but instead justify our charity. By giving much of what I have to the poor, I may develop attitudes to explain my behavior. For example, my attitude may be one of social hedonism, seeking the greatest good for the greatest number. Thus, I may conclude that all Christians should give more to the poor, thereby evoking resentment and division in the body of Christ.

Purchase power. Sleeping in on Saturdays is a luxury that Lisa and I cherish (sleeping in for us means getting up at 8:00 A.M. instead of 6: 00 A.M.) We often lie in bed on Saturday mornings chatting about our plans for the day. An interesting pattern has emerged. When we don't have definite plans, our discussion drifts toward shopping. We've made a lot of impulsive purchases on Saturdays: the racquetball shoes that were promptly stolen, giant coloring books for our daughters, hanging file folders so we can *someday* reorganize our files, the home computer, and so forth. Shopping on Saturdays is an enjoyable activity, but we must exercise caution to limit our shopping urges.

Americans at every income level, except the highest upper class, say they would be happier with 10 to 15 percent more income. We spend what we have and wish for more. In fact, many often spend more than they have and wish for more. An insightful limerick goes like this:

> A spendthrift fellow named Sy,
> Who charged everything he could buy,

> Said when hauled into court,
> With his bank account short,
> The government does, why can't I?

I was able to see the trap of consumerism very clearly while recently working with a Christian couple in marital therapy. Both had good incomes and yet they had made financial commitments that required them each to work sixty to seventy hours per week. They felt they were drifting in their marriage and their spiritual commitments to God. Reducing their work was not an option because of financial obligations. The subtle trap was spawned by meism. Making and spending more money consumed them and the broader aspects of God's truth were obscured in the process.

Doing orientation. A bright college student, Wendy was a pleasure to have in class. I was surprised one day by tears welling in her eyes as she began to discuss an upcoming test. Demands for perfection caused her great anxiety as she anticipated the midterm. She described a life busy with *doing* many things. Even as a five-year-old she was busy with ballet, gymnastics, theater, and music. Fighting back the tears, she said, "Everyone thinks I'm so self-confident, but I feel like I constantly have to win approval from others."

It's so natural to believe our worth depends on performance. What Wendy verbalized in my office goes on in the minds of most students and most employees and most everyone. Wendy had enough self-confidence to admit her feelings. We begin to think we are worthwhile only if we accomplish something outstanding. Not only do we value excellence, we hinge our identity on it.

Two cardiologists once noticed their office furniture wore out near the front of each chair. They discovered a personality characteristic causing their heart patients to sit on the edge of the chairs. Since that time there have been numerous research studies on the Type A personality pattern. Armed with a zeal for success, Type A individuals work competitively to complete tasks regardless of their importance. One Type A person said he found the secret to successful business was just working half days. He added, "The real beauty is, it doesn't matter which twelve hours you work."

Perhaps we work so hard because we need to prove our worth by *doing*. Prime-time television portrays worthwhile Americans as wealthy individualists, concerned for themselves first, who are enormously successful in all their endeavors.

God has no performance requirement before he will love us. It's a peaceful thought for a hectic world. His model is one of grace rather than performance.

Narcissism.   Another result of meism is narcissism, included as a psychiatric diagnosis for the first time in 1980. Symptoms of narcissism include a grandiose sense of self-importance, preoccupation with fantasies of success, requiring constant attention, and indifference to the feelings of others. One narcissistic couple whispering loudly in a movie theater was allegedly asked by a man behind to be more considerate because he could hardly hear. They replied, "You're not supposed to, this is a private conversation."

Psychologist Richard Kopelman and librarian Lynn Mullins conducted an analysis of nonfiction bestsellers for narcissistic content. They found a steady increase in narcissistic topics in published books from 1950 to 1980. In the midst of a society characterized by meism, narcissism is gaining ground.

The merchant's advice on "Little House on the Prairie" reflected a narcissistic worldview. "If it feels right to you, then it's right." This places self as ultimate authority and ignores any higher system of morality. Being in God's image must involve more than narcissism. It must involve searching beyond self to find truth.

Palliative coping strategies for dealing with duality have been considered in the last four chapters. Hiding Hyde makes our dual nature private so others will accept us. Conformity, aloneness, guilt, and greater duality result. Answerism involves suppressing the dark side, even from our own awareness and cloaking our glossy side in apparent rationality. It results in a form of righteousness that carries unnecessary bondage seen in defensiveness, rigidity, and self-justification. Hiding Jekyll suppresses innate notions of morality and looks to open sin as a solution. After the immediate pleasure, the sin solution becomes self-defeating, leading to self-centeredness and unsatisfactory relationships. Meism disguises dark-side impulses in rationality and seeks to please self. Unlike hiding Jekyll, morality is considered with meism but only from a narrow narcissistic perspective. All these strategies focus on self rather than on God's truth. They are impulsive strategies and ineffective ways of dealing with duality.

An alternative way of coping with duality is presented in the final chapters. Once we grasp the inevitability of duality, we begin to grow as we search for God's truth in the midst of discomfort. There is great freedom in the truth of God's grace.

> ...Who will set me free from the body of this death? Thanks be to God through Jesus Christ our Lord! So then, on the one hand I myself with my mind am serving the law of God, but on the other, with my flesh the law of sin. There is therefore now no condemnation for those who are in Christ Jesus. For the law of the Spirit of life in Christ Jesus has set you free from the law of sin and of death (Rom. 7:24–8:2).

9

Seeking Truth

Rather than love,
than money,
than fame,
give me truth.

Henry David Thoreau, *Walden*

So what is the answer to duality? On one hand, I have suggested there are no answers to duality. That is, we can never eliminate duality. On the other hand, the answer is found in admitting there are no answers. Once one gives up the frantic search for answers, there is freedom to seek truth. Truth seeking allows us to manage duality effectively. Thinking freely, we can move beyond trying to eliminate duality and consider the bigger issues in life. These "big" issues are considered in this final section. While not a solution to duality, truth seeking is the resource necessary to manage duality effectively.

Seeking happiness is a fitting analogy. Those who strive for happiness find it eludes them. Happiness can't be obtained directly. But those who seek meaning often find happiness in the process. So it is with duality.

Those trying to eliminate it do not succeed. Those seeking truth often manage duality effectively.

I will not attempt to describe what truth is, but will explore the implications of *seeking* truth. Our destination is not a set of facts called truth, but is freedom to pursue truth actively, to think openly, and to function rationally. Each of us labors, in the words of John Masefield, to build our ship of truth. Our ships become vehicles for exploring the substance of life. These ships are built with tools of love, pain, and hope—the tools needed in understanding truth. And well-built ships are guided with rudders of grace. Grace is a great truth.

Truth and Jell-O

Truth, like Jell-O, is slippery. We grab hold and it oozes through our fingers. For years the physical sciences accepted Newtonian physics as truth. But Einsteinian physics shattered many of Newton's theories. Theory is an imperfect human invention to better understand God's truth. The slipperiness of truth causes some to conclude it is a search only for super-intellectuals. But all of us have rational capacities and all can seek truth.

Showing truth to others is like posting Jell-O on a bulletin board. It disappears before our eyes. Just when we believe we have stumbled upon an important insight, we realize our insight is not understood by others. We may tend to retreat in defeat and leave the search for truth to somebody else.

Because truth is difficult, we sometimes resort to answerism. Some conclude scriptural truth is concrete and easy to understand, whereas philosophical or scientific truth is elusive and slippery. This is an unnecessary distinction, confusing principles with truth. For example, we point to a biblical commandment prohibiting stealing and claim it as truth. The commandment is a principle based on truth. It is not itself truth. The underlying truth is more general. For example:

Principle: I shouldn't steal.

Underlying truths: God is pleased by honesty and
                         not deception.
                         The rights of others are as significant as my own rights.

Truth requires rational thought and is often slippery, even truth found in the Bible. Answerism rarely does it justice.

This doesn't mean truth is relative. Since God created a world of order, truth follows order. It is absolute and guides nature. The truth of gravity, that two bodies attract each other, is difficult for a grade-school child to understand but it is nonetheless true and appears to have no exceptions. Not understanding truth does not compromise its status as absolute, so we keep exercising rationality in a never-ending pursuit of truth. This pursuit, the process of actively seeking truth, yields us rational beings fully capable of finding meaning in God's creation.

All Truth Is God's Truth

I loved to organize baseball cards as a child. First, I sorted my hundreds of cards into positions. All the catchers were in one pile, the right fielders in another, and so on. Then I ranked each position from the best player to the worst. My rankings were a subjective analysis based on whether the player had a good batting average and didn't chew too much tobacco. I then created my all-star team having selected, in my opinion, the best nine players in baseball.

Sometimes we approach truth in a similar way. First, we put truth in piles. The Bible is one pile of truth, science is another, literature yet another, and so forth. Then we rank order our piles. Since the Bible is inspired by God, it is the greatest truth. Science is a human endeavor so it is a lesser truth. Literature is just someone's opinion so it is near the bottom of our list.

Rank-ordering truth leads to difficulties. In 1615, the Church rejected the Copernican theory that the earth revolved around the sun because it was "unscriptural." Since the Bible supposedly said the sun revolves around the earth, scientific truth was rejected and biblical truth naively endorsed. Now we say they didn't interpret the Bible correctly, but we have the benefit of hindsight. How do we know we interpret the Bible correctly now when there is a conflict with science? Can we automatically assume the scientific theory of evolution is incorrect because we interpret the Bible to support creation? Rank-ordering truth can be deceptive.

Alternatively, we can view all truth as God's truth. Scripture and nature are data to be used in understanding truth better. Rank ordering isn't necessary. Science arrives at truth by experimentation. Theology arrives at truth by interpretation of Scripture. Literature arrives at truth by creatively analyzing human experiences. The variety of methods leads to different aspects of God's truth.

But what if science and theology are in opposition as they were in 1615? We have obviously interpreted one source of data incorrectly when such conflicts arrive. Either we have misinterpreted Scripture, as with the Copernican controversy, or we have misinterpreted scientific findings. By actively seeking truth (with an open mind) many of these controversies are resolved. After all the data are correctly interpreted, we will be closer to God's truth.

Sacred and Secular

I recently heard a Christian speaker explain that we can cure duality by giving up the music, literature, and entertainment of the world. Using James 4:7–10 as his text, he insisted that participation in these things causes us to be the enemy of God. But the context of the passage shows that self-centeredness (v. 2) is the worldly system James is condemning. This speaker's advice did the same thing as the worldly system James was condemning: it focused on self—what *I* can do to be a better Christian. Asceticism is no more spiritual than hedonism. Our objective is to draw near to God (v.8) and to spend less time thinking about self. Is the music, entertainment, and literature of the world the enemy? Perhaps. But so are the self-focused efforts of asceticism.

Because we sometimes rank order truth, we make artificial distinctions between the sacred and the secular. Because God inspired the Bible, it is sacred. Science and literature are taught in school, so they are secular. In his insightful essay *The Answer of Religion*, Alan Watts writes that religion "amounts virtually to the complete denial of life as we understand it."[1] He explains that Christians view the secular as a spiritual snare. Do we need to distinguish so carefully between the spiritual and the secular?

If all truth is God's truth, we need not make this distinction. Seeing truth through the eyes of a masterful writer can be a tremendous spiritual experience. Understanding the miraculous nature of God through scientific inquiry can bring glory to God.

Other aspects of existence (physical, emotional, mental) are defined very broadly while spirituality is often limited to a set of specified activities. We don't conclude a person is being emotional only if he or she is crying or yelling. Emotions occur in response to a beautiful sunset, a silly movie, or a touching song. Similarly, physical existence does not occur only when we run or lift weights. Back pain, nerve twitches, and hunger pangs are equally physical. Even the emotionally moving sunset results in subtle physical changes. But spirituality is sometimes defined by a very limited set of activities: church, Bible reading, and prayer. The beautiful sunset, the silly movie, the back pain, or the touching song can also be valuable *spiritual* experiences. We need not limit spirituality to specifically defined activities. All truth is God's truth.

Some value reading nonfiction (like this book) above reading fiction. One is growth producing and the other

1. Watts, Alan W. (1968). *The meaning of happiness*. New York: Harper & Row.

entertaining. But can't entertainment produce growth? Don't we better understand truth after reading the work of a perceptive fiction author?

In preparation for this book, I read Robert Louis Stevenson's, *The Strange Case of Dr. Jekyll and Mr. Hyde.* I didn't set the book down until I was done. My horizons were expanded in those few hours. Many concepts in this book were enhanced because of Stevenson's marvelous treatise which we consider to be a secular work of fiction.

One of my most spiritually enlightening experiences came while watching a movie that many Christians would refuse to watch because of the rating. As I watched the horrors of a Nazi concentration camp and a mother forced to choose between her two children, my world view was broadened and I understood more fully what suffering really is. The human dilemmas of hedonism and altruism and the potential for unthinkable evil were vividly painted on my memory and my understanding of God's grace expanded. Several years later, I continue to see that movie as a significant factor in my spiritual pilgrimage.

Of course many movies and books are spiritually dangerous. I am mindful of Paul's warning the Romans not to place stumbling blocks in the paths of others. We need sensitivity to our limits and others' limits.

Thought

Finding truth requires thought. The rational life motive, created in God's image, leads to understanding. Despite its great power and usefulness, many fear thought. Bertrand Russell, an English philosopher, wrote:

> Men fear thought as they fear nothing else on earth, more than death. Thought is subversive and revolutionary, destructive and terrible. Thought is merciless to privilege, established institutions, and comfortable habits. Thought looks into the pit of hell and is not afraid. Thought is great and swift and free, the light of the world and the chief glory of men.

Russell was outspoken in his opposition to Christianity. His book *Why I Am Not a Christian* suggested that Christians fear thinking. Could he be right?

In A.D. 180, the philosopher Celsus wrote of Christians:

> Their injunctions are like this. "Let no one educated, no one wise, no one sensible draw near. For these abilities are thought by us to be evils. But as for anyone ignorant, anyone stupid, anyone uneducated, anyone who is a child, let him come boldly."

Although he overstated it, maybe Celsus had a valid concern. Answers are easier than thought. By compiling a list of spiritual answers to life's problems we can spare the pain of thought. So answers come freely in Christianity. Dancing is wrong. Daily devotions are right. Smoking is wrong. Praying before meals is right. *G* rated movies are all right, but all others are sinful. The list goes on and on. The conclusions may be useful, but deriving the conclusions often involves little or no thought. It seems to be truth because the pastor said it or because we read it in a book by a Christian author.

Paul wrote that God made foolish the wisdom of the world. At first, this might seem to be an argument against thought. But remember the context. In 1 Corinthians 1:18 Paul stated the word of the cross is foolishness to those who are perishing. God's infinite grace, as evidenced by the sacrificial death of Christ, is foolishness to the world. The passage is about the miracle of God's grace, not a passage condemning thought. Paul himself was skilled in thought and used many rational arguments in his writings.

Thought is powerful. Some blame thought when their children go off to secular universities and abandon Christian faith. But did thinking lead them astray? Or could it be a result of nonthinking? Could it be we have failed to teach them to think Christianly with as much insight and integrity as the great thinkers in society? Perhaps the avoidance of thought creates the problems for Christians at secular universities. Emile Zola in *J'accuse* wrote, "If you shut up truth and bury it under the ground, it will but grow, and gather to itself such explosive power that the day it bursts through it will blow up everything in its way."

It is simplistic to say, as Celsus and Russell, that Christians avoid thought. Many Christians are great thinkers, willing to think about all issues. We need such thinkers.

In a back issue of *Christianity Today*[2] I found an article by Dean Merrill, editor of *Leadership* magazine. The article, entitled "The Sexual Hazards of Pastoral Care," dealt openly with the problem of sexual temptation for pastors. Many avoid this topic because we

2. *Christianity today.* November 8, 1985, 105.

already know the answer: adultery is wrong. But Mr.
Merrill is a thinker. He thought and wrote about this
tough issue without resorting to answerism. Yes, adultery is wrong, but how does a pastor deal with sexual
temptation?

Is any matter too sacred to evaluate with thought? I
think not. We need thinkers as much as we need answers.

Do We Need Permission to Think?

Shortly after writing a journal article on humanistic
psychology, I was handed a page titled, "Will you be
accused of teaching 'secular humanism'?" The page
included thirty questions including, "Do you ask students to clarify or examine their values?" "Do you ever
say to students that there are no right or wrong answers
to some questions?" and "Do you encourage your children to think critically?" At the bottom of this satirical
handout I was warned that I might be accused of teaching secular humanism if I answered yes to any of the
questions. In the witch hunt against secular humanism, Christians sometimes communicate that they oppose thought. Do we need God's permission to think?

Although I dislike the title, I teach secular humanism by these standards. I encourage my students to
think for themselves. I once had a class imagine there is
no God and to report their feelings about death. It was a
powerful faith-enriching experience, allowing students
to feel the hopelessness of atheism for a moment. Students don't leave my classes as humanists. They are
Christians with the ability to seek truth by thinking.

We don't need permission to question spiritual matters. Faith doesn't preclude thinking. In fact faith requires thinking. If our faith is true, it can withstand our thoughts. God's truth is credible enough to withstand careful scrutiny and evaluation. Abraham Maslow wrote:

> [Faith] in the hands of an anti-intellectual church tends to degenerate into blind belief...[which] tends to produce sheep rather than men...[When religion] was cut away from science, from knowledge, from further discovery, from the possibility of skeptical investigation, from confirming and disconfirming, and therefore from the possibility of purifying and improving, such a... religion was doomed.[3]

Maslow inappropriately elevates science above other ways of knowing in this statement, but his criticism deserves consideration. Is faith really faith if we avoid analyzing it skeptically? Or is it merely blind belief?

Another obstacle to some Christian thought is the high value placed on academic degrees. A pastor friend of mine was once told he could not speak at a certain church because only people with doctoral degrees were allowed to speak there. The degrees of a few may discourage many from doing their own thinking. "I'm not smart enough to understand these things." "I'll have to have my pastor explain this to me." Fresh, profound thoughts frequently come from the uneducated. Thinking doesn't require a degree.

Being new on the faculty at a Quaker college, their egalitarian emphasis surprised me. Having recently re-

3. Maslow, A.H. (1964). *Religions, values, and peak experiences.* Columbus: Ohio State University Press, 13–14.

ceived my graduate degree, I was disappointed to be called "Mr. McMinn" or "Mark" by students. Rarely did my ears feast in the vanity of "Dr. McMinn." This egalitarianism stuff devastated my pride at first. A few years older and wiser, I now encourage students and clients to use my first name. I love egalitarianism! Degrees have no spiritual significance. Truth comes from all sources, not just from "doctors." Some of the wisest, most insightful people on our campus work in the maintenance department.

Thinking may be improved with education, but don't assume great thinkers always have an education. Erik Erikson, a Christian and a psychological theorist, is one of the great thinkers of this century. Erikson has no college degree and no graduate degree but he has significantly influenced modern thought and has held faculty positions at prestigious universities. God gives the resources to think when he creates us in his image. He requires no degrees to activate those resources.

Beyond Defensiveness

Much truth seeking is personal. Being able to find and understand personal truth is of great value. Defensiveness is the enemy of personal truth. Palliative coping strategies, discussed in previous chapters, are defensive ways to disguise personal truth. Defenses relieve the pain of truth for a time. In his essays on intellect, Emerson wrote, "God offers to every mind a choice between truth and repose. Take which you please, you can never have both."

Duality is a personal truth and a universal truth. We experience conflicts of impulse and reason regularly.

Defenses—answerism, meism, hiding Hyde, hiding Jekyll—only provide brief repose and avoid truth.

Once we accept duality as truth, we begin to seek greater truths. Begin to ask, "How can I learn from this temptation?" instead of, "How can I avoid this?"

Cognitive Modification

David was married. But Cheryl, a colleague at work, didn't seem to mind. She kept after him anyway. David's commitment to marriage was strong and he seemed unconcerned about Cheryl at first. But she kept flirting, and he started to become interested. A cognitive therapist, I was interested in exploring David's thoughts. He felt terrible that he was tempted to be unfaithful. He wanted help to escape the temptation. Unfortunately, Cheryl seemed to follow him wherever he went and it seemed unlikely that he could escape the temptation. David's thoughts went something like this:

"It is awful that I am attracted to Cheryl."

"Cheryl is impossible to resist."

"I have to be faithful, but I can't keep from being unfaithful."

By helping David change his thoughts, I was able to reduce his stress. Instead of thinking how awful the temptation was, I had David reflect on the value of the temptation. What could he learn from this? How could it help him grow? David called a few months ago. Cheryl is gone now, and he remained faithful to his wife. In fact he said his marriage is stronger than ever.

Now he knows the price of fidelity. He exposed his belief to careful thought and now he believes it more than ever.

Changing two thought patterns about duality can move us beyond defensiveness, enabling us to better understand truth. First, it is useful to look for value in everything. Because I am part-time at a counseling center, I was once moved into the smallest office. This seemed negative until I realized I then had two windows in my office instead of one. Then I felt fine about switching offices because I was thinking differently about the event. Similarly, there is value in thinking positively about duality. Tempting impulses are not evil in themselves and can, in fact, cause me to grow as my commitment is tested. The true nature of marital commitment can't be fully experienced until temptation to violate that commitment arises. Temptation can be welcomed as an avenue of seeking truth.

Second, replace thoughts such as, "I can't stand it." Duality is uncomfortable because it never gives up. Some individuals battle with the same temptations over and over for years. It's natural to stomp our emotional feet and exclaim, "I can't handle this any longer." Remember Paul's words:

> No temptation has overtaken you but such as is common to man; and God is faithful, who will not allow you to be tempted beyond what you are able, but with the temptation will provide the way of escape also, that you may be able to endure it (1 Cor. 10:13).

David was attracted for many months to a woman actively attempting to seduce him. He learned from his

temptation and grew stronger in his marital commitment. He not only withstood the temptation, he prof-
ited from it. He found meaning in temptation and
transcended thoughts such as, "I can't stand it." In fact,
he later described the temptation as the most enriching
experience of his life.

A Case Study

Brian was filled with guilt and remorse. His short-
lived affair with Elise, a co-worker, nearly ended his
marriage and devastated his successful career. Brian, a
deep thinker and an articulate communicator, was almost unable to think rationally about spiritual issues.
A committed Christian, Brian learned all the answers
as a child but never bothered to *think* about dark-side
impulses. When those impulses came after four years of
marriage, Brian concluded he "couldn't stand it." After
leaving his wife and children, his guilt soon crushed his
independence and he returned home.

As a Christian counselor, Brian expected me to give
him some answers. He seemed surprised when I encouraged him to *think* about his feelings toward Elise.
Wasn't the Christian response to eliminate all
thoughts about her?

Several weeks later Brian explained that the relationship with Elise could have never worked. He wouldn't
be able to trust himself or her sufficiently for a long-
term relationship. The conclusion, although obvious to
an outside observer, was the product of Brian's own
thinking. With tears in his eyes, Brian told me he
hadn't thought about the consequences of having an
affair because he felt guilty for even thinking of Elise.

My permission several weeks earlier had started him thinking rationally of the consequences.

I could have given Brian the same conclusion (in the form of an answer) on our first session. Instead I gave him permission to think. As a result, he came to the conclusion. Brian learned from his sin and now thinks honestly about dark-side impulses without irrational guilt. I couldn't take away his pain. His feelings for Elise were very deep. But his pain had meaning as he sought truth.

A Narrow Fence

Thinking about impulse is like walking on a narrow fence. Caution and balance are essential because the fence separates two extremes. On one side of the fence, impulses are avoided altogether, resulting in answer-ism and defensiveness. On the other side of the fence, a person might think about impulses so much that the thoughts become sinful fantasy. This chapter has only focused on one side of the fence—the side where impulse is not allowed. Speaking of a recurrent temptation, a client recently told me, "I don't want to hassle with it; I just want to feel good and comfortable and safe." In her defensiveness and covering of impulse she had resorted to hiding Hyde and was experiencing stress-related physical problems as a result.

We must also consider the other side of the fence. In thinking too much about temptations, we may slip into patterns of sin. Paul told Timothy to flee youthful lusts and pursue righteousness. In his Sermon on the Mount, Jesus taught that thoughts could be as sinful as actions.

How can we walk the fence, allowing ourselves to evaluate temptation without slipping into sin?

Distinguishing between self-centeredness and truth-centeredness is useful. Self-centered thoughts regarding temptations, including fantasies of pleasure or power, make falling off the fence likely. "When lust has conceived, it gives birth to sin; and when sin is accomplished, it brings forth death" (James 1:15). Truth-centered thoughts about temptation are productive and prevent future sin. Truth-centered thoughts might include:

1. What has led me into this temptation?
2. What would be the consequences of this action?
3. What moral principles apply here and why?
4. How does this help me better understand others?
5. How does this help me better understand God?
6. How does this help me better understand truth?

Liberation in Seeking Truth

After considering the ideas in this chapter for several weeks, a client stated, "I feel so free; I wish I could help others at the church see this." There is a liberation in thinking.

Truth seeking goes far beyond answerism. Shortly after talking to the answer-oriented Pharisees, Jesus announced that abiding in his word results in knowing truth. "...You shall know the truth, and the truth shall make you free" (John 8:32). Jesus went on to explain that he has power over the bondage of sin. Just compare the lifestyles. The Pharisees were in bondage, and Jesus was free. He lived a spontaneous life filled with meaning and truth.

Later the church again became stifled by answers. Martin Luther championed a reform focusing on freedom in God's truth. Could this be a repetitive cycle? As evangelicalism moves toward answerism, let's remember the liberation of God's truth.

Do we really experience the freedom of his grace? Defensive strategies limit freedom by limiting God's truth. Seeking truth is liberating. We don't always find truth because some supercedes human comprehension. Some questions are too big for answers, as indicated in chapter 7, but asking questions and seeking truth are valuable nonetheless.

10

Seeking Personal Truth

> To thine own self be true,
> And it must follow, as the night the day,
> Thou canst not then be false to any man.
>
> Shakespeare, *Hamlet, I, 3.*

A great imposter throughout his life, Fred Demara took on the identity of a Trappist monk, a Latin teacher, a cancer researcher, a military surgeon, and a psychology professor. Actually he was a high-school dropout. Deciding against becoming an actor, he commented that acting seemed "too artificial." Demara spent much of his life searching for identity, never embracing who he was in reality. His was an identity crisis.

Duality creates identity crises for Christians. Paul put it well when he wrote, ". . .that which I am doing, I do not understand; for I am not practicing what I would like to do, but I am doing the very thing I hate" (Rom. 7:15). Apart from God's grace, which Paul considered in Romans 8, he was unsure of his identity. Since duality can never be eliminated, traces of confused identity remain for Christians. But as we fully embrace ourselves, including our impulses and our

149

rationality, and understand God's character we begin to gain a greater sense of identity.

Trying to eliminate duality keeps us from fully knowing ourselves because duality is part of our identity. But self-awareness is risky. Assume Mr. M. Pulse, a typical growing Christian, has learned to accept himself and recognize his impulses. He confides in a Christian friend, telling of his tendency to act aggressively toward his children. Concerned, Mr. Pulse's friend recommends he get spiritual help. Feeling misunderstood, Mr. Pulse sinks back into duality, convinced that self-acceptance results in rejection from others. His sense of identity is again distorted.

Congruence and Christianity

"Congruent" is how Carl Rogers described a healthy psychological state. A congruent person has a clear sense of identity without denial or distortion.

Critics of psychology have noted the incompatibility of some of Rogers' writings with scriptural teaching, but we don't have to agree with all of Rogers' theory or personal philosophy to profit from his concept of congruence.

Seeing ourselves accurately is biblical. In his book *The Christian Looks at Himself*, Anthony Hoekema provides biblical support for a healthy self-image. Many Christians disagree. In a videotape lecture, a popular Christian counselor insists that Christians should not have a self-image. Instead, he suggests, we should look to God for our identity. How can anyone *not* have a self-image? It's like not seeing our faces when we look in the mirror. Whether we like it or not, our faces are there, staring back at us. Not perceiving ourselves is impossible. Hoekema constructs his biblical argument for self-esteem by carefully evaluating the apostle Paul.

This chapter will seem self-centered to some. I emphasize self-understanding and personal identity because these are part of seeking truth. Accurate self-understanding is truth-centered rather than self-centered. When Jesus warned to take the log out of one's own eye before attempting to remove the speck from another's, he advocated self-awareness.

Seeking personal truth goes far beyond self-acceptance. A major problem among some Christian groups is a lack of other-acceptance. We split denominations because we can't get along. Countless numbers of churches have ongoing factions on an everyday basis.

Other-acceptance has many implications. I frequently hear of those who desperately need counseling but won't see a Christian therapist because of the answerism they have received from church members. Many long for acceptance but get answers instead. Why? Perhaps we don't accept our brothers and sisters because we don't understand ourselves. James suggested that poor coping with personal impulses causes conflicts in our churches (James 4:1). The faults we identify in others are often the very faults we struggle to bury in ourselves, just as Jimmy Swaggart fought to control his own sexual sin while criticizing Jim Bakker's sexual sin.

Freud called it "reaction formation." Being outspoken and zealous is often a way to cope with our neurotic anxiety, warning us unconsciously of our vulnerability. An irate woman called the police department, reporting that young people were driving too fast in her neighborhood. The police promptly followed up and issued their first ticket. Surprisingly, the woman making the report received the citation. Her criticism of the young drivers in her neighborhood reflected her own struggles with impulse control. Our acceptance of others depends a great deal on self-acceptance. A tool in seeking truth is congruence: seeing ourselves accurately without distortions pushing us into palliative coping strategies and battles of impulse.

Incongruence in Palliative Coping

Distortion is used to protect us from negative parts of ourselves. Sampling five distortion strategies, first noted by Sigmund and Anna Freud, will demonstrate how palliative coping strategies result from incongruence.

Denial. This is refusing to perceive negative aspects of ourselves. Alexander C. De Jong wrote, "Denial is the shield used to protect one's inner self from the truth. It is a devastatingly effective means of clinging to feelings of self-worth while effectively committing suicide...." De Jong's insightful statement demonstrates that denial detracts from the search for personal truth.

One student wrote on a course evaluation form that I cared too much about what students think of me. At first I laughed it off as a ridiculous criticism from an insecure student. But as I reflected on the evaluation, I began to recognize my denial. I *did* care a lot about students' opinions. Perhaps this bold student was insightful rather than insecure. As this example illustrates, denial evokes the answer-oriented glossy side. With denial, the glossy side grows in order to repress the faults seen in the dark side.

Projection. This is placing blame on others for one's own impulses or faults. A study of college students showed that those who rate peers as stingy and obstinate are themselves stingy and obstinate. One client insisted she had to discontinue a friendship because her friend was so jealous of her. Later in the interview she stated that her friend had just been promoted at work, had just obtained a wonderful boyfriend, and was very successful financially. Who was jealous of whom? Projection often leads to the palliative coping strategy of meism. If others have these negative qualities (that are really my qualities), then I must protect myself so I am not burned by their jealousy or stinginess or obstinacy. Meism is thereby rationally justified.

Rationalization. This is similarly attempting to prove a behavior is justifiable by producing well-reasoned arguments. This common defense easily leads to meism or answerism, depending on whether the dark side or the glossy side is being rationalized. Impulsive motives can easily be disguised in costumes of rationality.

Undoing. This is compensating for dark-side impulses with some act of atonement. A husband bringing home flowers after meeting his clandestine mistress for lunch is an example. Undoing escalates duality by hiding Hyde. Some "spiritual" activities may be ways to compensate for undesirable impulses.

Acting out. This reduces the anxiety aroused by dark-side desires by permitting their expression. Restraints are abandoned. Acting out is incongruent because it denies our innate sense of morality and rationality. Hiding Jekyll results.

These are just five of many defense strategies. A clear connection between defense patterns and palliative coping strategies can be seen with each.

A congruent person recognizes personality accurately. Rationality controls but impulses are recognized without distortion. All impulses, both from the glossy side and the dark side, are embraced as tools for learning and evaluated through the filter of rationality. Walls between impulse and rationality become unnecessary because both coexist in an environment where impulse is managed effectively.

Becoming Congruent

Figure 12 illustrates congruence. Rather than walling off rationality with battles of impulse, both motives coexist. Because rationality is not walled off, it is part of the decision-making process. Dark-side impulses are accepted and rationally evaluated. Glossy-side impulses are also acknowledged. Guilt from the glossy side and urges from the dark side are not overwhelming because they are processed with rationality. Congruence results in self-awareness without need for defense or palliative coping strategies. Of course, some tension remains because the congruent person does not hope to eliminate duality, only to manage it.

How does one become congruent? Here are some ideas that may be useful in seeking personal truth.

Accepting impulses. Some defensiveness results from guilt which, in turn, results from impulse. For example, I might have a fleeting impulse to play golf on Sunday morning instead of going to church. Guilt might result immediately from such an impulse. Guilt might then generate distortions and incongruence. If hiding Hyde was my inclination, I might tell myself that good Christians don't ever struggle with the temptation to play golf on Sundays and that I am surely the biggest hypocrite of all time. To compensate, I get up immediately and have devotions before I go to church (undoing). If meism was my tendency, I might persuade myself that I need the leisure time and wouldn't be able to worship anyway, so I might as well play golf. After all, I'm worth it (rationalization).

Figure 12 Congruent state: Impulses are accepted and evaluated openly. No walls exist.

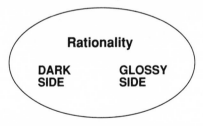

Feeling guilty for impulses is unproductive. Impulses are not wrong until they give birth to sin (James 1:15). If, instead of feeling guilty, I accept my impulse to play golf and evaluate it rationally, I avoid defensiveness. Rationally, I affirm the value of meeting with others for Christian fellowship. Or perhaps my five-year-perfect-attendance pin (glossy side) isn't as important as I think, and the golfing impulse reminds me that approval needs are not sufficient motivation for church attendance.

Remember that impulses are not evil just as temptation is not evil. Choosing to behave sinfully in response to an impulse is another matter. Why do I work so hard at making this point in several different chapters? Because impulses can add great vitality to life. Spontaneously doing something "crazy" can greatly benefit one's mental health. Deciding at the last minute to go to the beach for the weekend, choosing the more expensive dress just because it looks better, and selecting the New York steak instead of the diet plate can all be appropriate, even though they result from impulse. Many times these are not issues of sin but issues of choice. To live life denying all impulse is to miss much joy of spontaneity.

Similarly, glossy-side impulses to consider the opinions of others are healthy in mild doses. The opinions of others keep us socially appropriate. In the midst of a hot June commencement service, I would like to take off my faculty robe, roll up my sleeves, and take a nap. But I don't because it would be socially inappropriate. Little rationality is involved; impulse keeps me from doing these things. Impulses, per se, are not evil. They can add joy to life as we accept them as part of ourselves.

Identifying emotions.   As I mentioned in chapter 2, selecting the word *rationality* to contrast with impulse was difficult because rationality has negative connotations. When I think of a rational person I think of a Certified Public Accountant with wire-framed glasses sitting in front of ledger sheets while the family opens Christmas presents. To the extent that rationality implies sterile cognition, it is a misnomer. Rationality, as I intend it, also includes sensitivity to emotional and intuitive experiences. Emotions are as real as thoughts and have the potential to be equally valuable.

Congruence involves accepting emotions. The same speaker who said Christians shouldn't have self-images also said we feel anger because we have self-images—if we give up our self-image, we will no longer feel angry. But that's not biblical. Jesus got angry. Paul told the church at Ephesus to be angry, but not to sin (Eph. 4:26). If anger were a sin, this would be an impossible command.

Deep inside our brains is the limbic system, a neural pathway causing the experience of emotion. Anger, passivity, and sexuality are drastically affected by the activities of these neural tissues. Would God program us to experience anger and then condemn it as sin? Is it reasonable to feel guilt for a biologically caused impulse?

Even emotions can be analyzed rationally. Looking for the origin of the emotions, evaluating how reasonable the emotion is, and investigating the consequences are truth-seeking processes. Even labeling emotion is an important rational function. Many Christians are so guilt-ridden about emotions that they do not know what they are feeling. I sometimes have clients list the different emotions experienced during the coming week. They often come back with three emotions: *happy*, *sad*, and *mad*. I then send them back to their feelings with a goal of finding seventy-five. It sounds like a lot, but we have many human feelings: *hungry, tired, bored, irritated, frustrated, nauseous, excited*, and so forth.

Rationality involves more than sterile thinking. A congruent person also recognizes feelings accurately. Defensively denying feelings results in distortions of identity.

Being, not doing.   Society values doing so much that we begin to identify who we are with what we do. Congruence needs a broader base of identity. For example, if I yell at my child, I will feel guilty. My *doing* was evil, therefore I am evil. I might then hide my dark side because telling others of my failure would reveal my worthlessness. If worth is based on performance, I cannot see myself as unconditionally accepted. But God's love *is* unconditional. He sees our *being* and not our doing. As we shift our emphasis from doing to being, from glossy to rational, we strive less to eliminate duality and we are better able to seek personal truth.

Humor.   Lee Trevino once said that if his IQ was any lower he would be a plant. Being able to laugh at ourselves requires congruence. Those who are defensive or uncomfortable about weaknesses aren't able to laugh about them without seeking reassurance from others.

I used to laugh about having a long nose, but it was mostly a strategy for reassurance. People were supposed to say my nose looked fine. I was shattered one day when someone asked if I knew how to make my nose six inches long. He answered by saying, "fold it in half." I stopped laughing about my nose.

Laughing honestly about our weaknesses or impulses fosters congruence. Impatience with noise is one of my weaknesses. Having three young children at home, I get my share of noise and occasionally resort to some impulsive verbal noise of my own to reduce theirs. Sometimes when the noise level gets ear splitting, Lisa (who knows of my tendency to yell, "Silence!") looks at me and smiles. Laughter in her eyes helps me gain perspective, and we chuckle together for a few moments about the plight of parenting. The noise seems more manageable after those brief periods of laughter, and I recognize that noise isn't as bad as my impulses would have me believe.

Welcoming evaluation.   We often fear others evaluating us, perhaps because it is occasionally painful. But evaluation provides greater opportunity for congruence. Seeing ourselves through the eyes of others helps us know ourselves better. "Iron sharpens iron, so one man sharpens another" (Prov. 27:17).

Teachers hate student evaluations. But they are often quite useful, allowing us to improve teaching methods. After getting over the sting of criticism, I have routinely asked students to evaluate my courses, even though the dean requires evaluations only once a year. Evaluations are useful to me, not only in understanding my teaching methods, but in understanding myself.

The opinions of others provide valuable insights into ourselves. Impulsive persons dismiss them as pointless or irrelevant. Congruent persons carefully consider them, not because of approval needs but to see themselves more accurately.

Self-disclosure.   My five-year-old daughter once suggested a way to share a Life Saver. "I suck it for a while, then you suck it for a while, then I suck it some more...." Although a disgusting way to share Life Savers, her model is useful for sharing impulses. Sharing impulses with another makes them seem smaller just as a communal Life Saver becomes smaller and smaller.

Hiding Hyde produces profound aloneness. "No one experiences the impulses I do." "I am the worst of all sinners." Congruence can't be obtained in the midst of such self-condemnation. But disclosing impulses to others disconfirms many self-condemning thoughts. We begin to realize that impulses are normal and do not indicate deviance of character.

For example, most (perhaps all) people feel attractions outside of marriage from time to time. Fewer feel free to share these attractions with their spouses. This privacy can be rationalized out of concern for the spouse. "It would only worry her to know," seems at first a reasonable conclusion. But often the privacy is really a defensive strategy. I suspect sexual temptation rarely turns into an affair when the spouse is informed when the attraction is first noticed.

Self-disclosure is good, but indiscriminate self-disclosure can be dangerous. Jim and Marilyn came for counseling on the verge of divorce. Jim had had many secret affairs in their three and a half years of marriage, but Marilyn finally found out about Jim's most recent lover. He responded by dumping all the details of his previous affairs onto her fragile psyche. She was shattered by his impulsive way of punishing her with excessive detail. Sometimes self-disclosure can be an obstacle rather than a help in reaching congruence. This will be discussed more later.

Obstacles to Congruence

Even after reaching congruence, it is easy to slip back into defensive patterns and incongruence. Maintaining congruence is a lifelong process with many obstacles.

Cognitive Distortions. Faulty thinking is an obstacle to congruence. Distorting reality with inaccurate thoughts produces poor self-management. Look for some "red flags" indicating cognitive distortion (inaccurate thinking). Many of these distortions are described more fully in Dr. David Burn's excellent book, *Feeling Good.*

Always is usually a cognitive distortion. If I tell myself I am always strong in the face of temptation, I am set up for failure because we all have moments of weakness. Likewise, if I tell myself I always give in to a certain temptation, it is a self-fulfilling distortion that overlooks times of victory.

Mind reading is another red flag. Mind reading is assuming the thoughts of another can be understood accurately. Let's assume I drag myself out of bed on that Sunday morning I wanted to go golfing. With bags under my eyes I eat my Cap'n Crunch and trudge to church. Sitting in the pew, I realize I forgot to shave. Immediately I begin to mind read. When others glance at me I assume they notice the dark circles and the unshaved chin. Surely they are assuming I have a hangover from a Saturday-night party. Concerned about my public image, I sink further into duality.

Should is a third red flag. Remember that *shoulds* are glossy-side impulses unless they are backed up with *whys*. Should statements often come as self-condemnation for impulse: "I shouldn't think those thoughts"; or "I shouldn't be concerned about my appearance." These things would be nice, but *shoulds* are too strong.

Fortune telling can lead to incongruence by predicting doom. Clients sometimes tell me they are anticipating a temptation and know they are not strong enough to handle it—fortune telling by predicting weakness. By viewing themselves as weak and helpless to temptation, they become weak.

Personalization is assuming fault for the difficulties of someone else. It is the opposite of projection. A Christian song I recently listened to implies the husband of an unfaithful wife is responsible since he is the head of the home. This exemplifies personalization. Is it reasonable to hold a husband responsible for the secret behaviors of his wife?

Labeling is perhaps the most subtle of the cognitive distortions. Attaching a label to ourselves can be misleading. Because you struggle with one temptation, you might label yourself weak. Since you perceive yourself to be weak, you may then begin to struggle with many other temptations. Labeling can thereby lead to incongruence.

Reactivity in others.   The reactions of others is a second obstacle to congruence. If self-disclosure is met with judgment, incongruence often results.

Wanda is becoming congruent. She is recognizing her impulses and attempting to deal with them rationally. She recognizes a sexual attraction to Ned, her next-door neighbor and close friend. Rather than feeling guilty, she attempts to understand herself better by evaluating the impulse. She soon realizes that much of her attraction is a result of Ned's complimentary manner. He always has something nice to say and makes her feel worthwhile. Wanda then identifies her need for approval and looks for other ways of coping with the need. In the process of dealing with her attraction rationally, Wanda tells her husband, Jon, about the situation. Feeling personally threatened, Jon instructs Wanda to keep her distance from Ned and begins looking through the Yellow Pages for a realtor. Jon has reacted to Wanda's self-disclosure by resorting to answerism.

Jon's reactivity will probably push Wanda away from congruence. She might agree with Jon and attempt to stay away from Ned altogether. But her impulses will remain and over time she may pick up the phone to call Ned. Once that happens, she will already feel like a sinner and more intense involvement with Ned may follow. Alternatively, she might disagree strongly with Jon's reactivity and respond by justifying her attraction to Ned, pushing her toward greater involvement with Ned.

Self-disclosure is appropriate, but choosing someone who will not overreact to the disclosure is important. Sometimes a spouse is too involved to keep from reacting, as with Jon and Wanda. Self-disclosure met with judgment in others makes congruence difficult to maintain. It is important to recognize limits in self-disclosure.

Congruent Relationships

Disclosing dark-side impulses to others often evokes glossy-side impulses in them as illustrated with Wanda and Jon. But when self-disclosure doesn't evoke reactivity, congruence is increased. In congruent relationships both persons can disclose impulses without evoking judgment in the other. These rational-to-rational relationships have several distinctives.

Listening. Listening is essential to congruent relationships. Nietzsche wrote, "A matter that becomes clear ceases to concern us." Perhaps Jon would have handled Wanda's revelation better had he listened before reacting.

Ironically, it is often difficult to listen to those closest to us—family members. One female author noted that before marriage a man will lie awake all night thinking about something you said, but after marriage he'll fall asleep before you finish saying it.

In listening, we sometimes assume too much, expecting that our interpretation is the same as the speaker's intent. But there are several layers to any communication.

Layer 1: The speaker's intent

Layer 2: The speaker's words

Layer 3: What the listener hears

Layer 4: Interpretation of speaker's intent

I may ask Lisa how long it will be until dinner is ready, hoping to have fifteen minutes to finish a project. If she assumes I am pressuring her to cook faster, she may feel frustration. What I meant (layer 1) and what she heard (layer 4) are very different. According to Goethe, "No one would talk much in society if he only knew how often he misunderstood others."

Reflection is a useful tool in active listening. The listener, by paraphrasing the message and saying it back, communicates a desire to understand accurately the intent of the message. Lisa might ask, "Are you in a hurry for dinner?" I could then explain my question more fully, preventing any conflict or resentment. In teaching counseling, I have students interview one another in my presence. While they talk, I count the number of reflections used. The more reflections, the higher I grade them. Reflecting does two things. First, it insures accurate listening. Second, it prevents giving too much advice.

Avoiding Advice Giving.   Uninvited advice giving is rarely seen in congruent relationships because it introduces power. Power, in turn, evokes impulse in the other. When Jon resorted to advising, he took a power position over Wanda. She was, for those few moments, like his daughter, employee, or pet. Jon's power evoked rebellion in Wanda, strengthening her impulse and destroying her efforts at congruence.

Parents of troubled adolescents struggle with this. The more they introduce power, the more the adolescent rebels. But as the rebellion continues, parents feel greater need for restraint, so they introduce more power, creating a vicious cycle.

Advice is fine when invited, and many answers are useful. Unwanted advice is rarely useful. Congruent relationships avoid advice giving.

Nonjudgmental. Congruent relationships are also nonjudgmental, absent of ridicule or belittlement. I've already stated that judgment is a result of impulse. Persons in congruent relationships seek truth together and avoid impulse.

Nonjudgment is particularly difficult in marriages after one person has been unfaithful. For example, one woman I worked with had continued contact with her former lover at work. Daily her husband asked about the interactions of the day. I tried to keep him from asking for that information, and he did a beautiful job of allowing her to volunteer the information, refraining from making judgmental observations or recommendations. His open-mindedness and willingness to withhold judgment resulted in great healing and growth in the relationship.

Part of avoiding judgment is keeping delicate information confidential within the congruent relationship. The judgment of others is prevented by maintaining confidentiality.

Congruent parenting. Since parents need to help children change inappropriate behaviors, it is more difficult to maintain congruent relationships. Sometimes parents give advice when it would not be appropriate in another relationship. But several principles are useful in raising congruent children.

First, *children need to have their own identities.* Each child is a unique combination of interests, abilities, and emotions. Attempting to mold a child into a lawyer, a neurosurgeon, or a homemaker overlooks the complexities of uniqueness. On the wall of our house hangs the adage,

> There are but two bequests we can give our children;
> one is roots,
> the other wings.

As children gain wings they learn the freedom to choose. Children deprived of choice find subtle ways to exercise choice. They make their choices when parents aren't looking and duality grows as congruence shrinks.

Joan, a sixteen-year-old teenager, was the apple of her mother's eye. Despite the rebellion of her older brother, Joan had always been the perfect girl. At least her mother thought so. It came as a surprise when Joan dropped school and left with her boyfriend for Nevada. When she returned several weeks later, her mother brought her for counseling. Joan was never the perfect girl her mother had thought. Her mother demanded perfection, so Joan developed a sophisticated glossy side. But late at night, she frequently sneaked from her bedroom window to spend the night with her boyfriend or go to a wild party. The Jekyll/Hyde syndrome was full-blown at age sixteen.

Second, *discuss temptations with your children.* Dr. James Dobson suggests parents should discuss the struggles of adolescence with their children. Dobson recommends preparing for temptation rather than denying it. Another example is teaching small children how to respond if approached by strangers. We drilled our children on this until it became routine. The stranger's piece of candy might be too tempting for the unprepared child.

Overpreparing is the other extreme. Children constantly warned of the big bad world will experience unnecessary anxiety about independence.

Third, *allow children to be sexual.* All humans are sexual, including children. Think for a moment about the paradox of sexuality in our Christian culture. Children are often taught that sexual urges are wrong. Adolescents often learn that sexuality, including all petting and masturbation, is sinful. On the wedding day, a person is magically transformed from asexual to sexual. After a glorious newlywed season, the troubles change. Married adults are informed that *not being sexual* is awful. Couples not having sex on a regular basis are told their marriage is not adequate. Sex is a confusing topic because we seem so hesitant to allow for individual differences.

Children are sometimes denied sexuality because parents fear the consequences. "If I allow my four-year-old to handle his genitals, he might become too sexual later on." "If my teenager is involved in masturbating or petting, premarital intercourse is sure to follow." But these are assumptions. Prohibiting sexuality causes duality to grow because kids are going to be sexual, whether it is allowed or not. The adolescent who is "sinning already" by petting or masturbating is more inclined to go ahead and "sin big" with premarital intercourse.

Watch for the other extreme also! We don't need to encourage sexual development in our children. My guess is that children are being exposed to more sexual immorality than ever before because of VCRs and video rentals. Time will tell if this is damaging to children's sexual development. I suspect it will be.

Parenting is not easy under the best circumstances. I have no formula for raising congruent children, but I prioritize three ideas as I struggle with the challenge of parenting. *Allowing children to be themselves, preparing them for temptations*, and *allowing appropriate sexuality* are useful tools to build congruent parent-child relationships.

Let's review briefly. There is no solution to the problem of duality, and trying to eliminate it makes things worse by starting a battle of impulses. Battles of impulse make us self-centered and prevent rational activity. By seeking truth (rational life motive) we avoid battles of impulses, keep duality in control, and move beyond self-centeredness.

Discovering truth begins on a personal level. Honestly recognizing who we are and putting aside defensiveness are essentials in seeking personal truth. As we strive for personal truth, we move beyond answerism and begin to evaluate bigger issues, causing growth and understanding. These bigger issues are considered in the final four chapters. Managing duality depends on understanding love, pain, hope, and grace.

11

Seeking Truth in Love

Ask not of me, love, what is love?
Ask what is good of God above—
Ask of the great sun what is light—
Ask what is darkness of the night—

Philip James Bailey, *Festus*

Dealing with duality is best done by disengaging ourselves from battles of impulse and then seeking truth. Seeking truth often involves asking important questions and contemplating their significance. One "big question" is, "What is love?" As Bailey wrote, love defies human definition. Only God, the author of love, can understand it completely. But struggling with the question, "What is love?" requires seeking truth and moving beyond the egocentrism of impulse. Limited views of love lead to greater duality.

Dana had not learned to understand love in her thirty-five years. She believed love and sex were identical. Even casual encounters with men ended up in her bedroom. Her impulsive style of love drove her to greater duality. Although she had lived on her own for almost twenty years, she couldn't tell her parents about her boyfriends. In fact, her parents thought her morally conventional. Her romantic impulses continued as the gulf grew between her hidden half and persona. She improved with counseling, not because of any great insights of mine, but because she was able to have a caring nonsexual relationship with a male for the first time. She began to explore her own motives and conflicts in past love relationships.

Defining Love

Asking ten people to define love would probably result in ten different answers. Many answers would share common elements, but they would also have distinct characteristics. There is no concensus on what love is.

An experience beyond definition. A May 6, 1985, *Newsweek* carried the story of a mysterious love. Fumiko Kimura, a native Japanese, drowned her two children in the ocean off Santa Monica, California, and then attempted to kill herself. What appeared to be a violent antisocial act in the USA was consistent with a Japanese tradition. In Japan, a woman who commits suicide without her children is condemned as evil. Killing one's children before killing oneself is honorable. Did Kimura love her children? To some, murdering her children means she didn't love them. To others, the drowning was love's evidence. Defining love depends on personal values and cultural perspectives.

We come to different conclusions depending on our

definitions. For example, is it sinful for a married woman to be in love with her husband and with another
man at the same time? Lisa concluded *yes*, and I concluded *no* after a lengthy debate (we enjoy philosophical debates), but we recognized the difference was with
our definition of love. She defines marital love as a
commitment to the relationship excluding other loves,
whereas I think of love and commitment as separate
events. Using her definition, I agree with her conclusion. Depending on how we define love, we derive
different conclusions about the nature of love.

Even without attempting to perfectly define love, we
can describe its characteristics.

Love is irreducible.   In efforts to define love, it is
often equated with other experiences. Some insist love
is a feeling. "Love Boat" perspectives say one can "fall"
in love at first sight and fall out of love equally fast.

I used this definition in junior high. I was sure I loved
my first girlfriend. When the feelings became overwhelming, I asked my friend to ask her friend if she
liked me. Word came back that she did and so I had a
girlfriend, for about a month. I smiled at her from
across the room and said, "Hi," when we saw each
other in the hall. My parents told me I couldn't really be
in love, but I didn't agree. Her feelings changed a month
later, and she told her friend to tell my friend she didn't
like me anymore. Junior high is difficult. My life
seemed destined to be a series of one-month relationships. The problem was my view of love.

Others view love as an action. They insist feelings
make no difference, that we love by performing loving

actions. This definition is better, but also has limits. If love is only an action, then love requires action. For example, if I was locked in a penitentiary and could not *do* anything for my spouse, would I then not love her? Clearly, I could still love my spouse even though I couldn't participate in loving actions.

I used to describe love as a way of thinking. But defining love as thought is also limited. At times my thoughts toward Lisa are not loving. Am I then "out of love"? Love must transcend feelings, actions, and thoughts.

Love is irreducible. It can't be explained as thought, action, or feeling. An existential phenomenon, love can only be experienced. Sure, love involves actions, thoughts, and feelings, but love cannot be reduced to these three. Love cannot be explained by any formula. It is irreducible.

Love is confusing. Confusion often leads to self-destructive behaviors which, in turn, often lead to marital counseling. Sometimes one spouse, caught in the midst of an affair, feels hopelessly out of control. Sometimes couples claim they have "fallen out of love." Other times couples complain that the vitality is gone. Many conclude that love is the enemy and married persons the victims.

Love is like the ocean. An idealistic teenager, I enjoyed thoughtfully watching the endless procession of ocean waves embrace the shore. Thoughts—often thoughts of love—flowed freely as I pondered the infinite power of God revealed in predictable swells of water and salt. But the ocean isn't always predictable. Wielding awesome power to destroy, the ocean is capable of causing turmoil and pain. The crash of a tidal wave or the tragedy of an untimely undertow can sap life at any instant. The apparent peace of the ocean is coupled with imminent danger.

Love is like the ocean. Its potential for peace and tranquility is easily shattered by its ominous destructive capacity. Love can cause joy or despair. Love is sometimes ripped apart by death. One partner dies unexpectedly, and the survivor is left with bittersweet memories and deep pain. Love that caused joy yesterday causes despair today. Paradoxically, we seek love but it causes pain.

Mature love helps us seek truth. Both partners strive to understand as conflicts and turmoils arise. Growth and understanding result as partners wrestle with the pain and joy of evolving love. But some loves miss these opportunities for growth.

Erik Erikson hypothesized that an intimate love relationship is impossible without first having a clear sense of identity. The congruent individual is more likely to experience meaningful love. Dr. Beatriz Dujoven writes:

Mature love can flourish only between two people who feel whole and worthwhile as individuals. Love is not possible when one partner is expected to fill the other's inner voids. "If you really loved me, you wouldn't need other people" is another expression of the desire to achieve the fusion we experienced with our mothers as babies.

We can distinguish impulsive love from transcendent love in a similar way. Impulsive love results from personal incongruence and is self-seeking. Transcendent love between congruent individuals goes beyond impulse and explores truth. Impulsive love avoids the difficult questions whereas transcendent love embraces them as opportunities for growth.

Impulsive Love

Bob was angry about coming for marriage counseling. His church elders insisted he come with Pat because their relationship had been full of turmoil since Bob's affair eighteen months before. Pat appeared motivated to work on the marriage. Her cool, rational style sharply contrasted Bob's anger. As we began, a discrepancy in goals became clear. Bob wanted a convenience marriage, to remain with Pat to keep the kids and have the security of two incomes. He didn't want Pat. He still loved his mistress of eighteen months ago. Pat, however, wanted closeness and intimacy. As she pressed for intimacy, he pressed for distance.

Bob's self-centeredness frustrated me. His efforts were impulsive and rarely rational, and predictably, he made little progress. In contrast, Pat grew in counseling. Mostly impulsive at first, her world view broadened. After six months of counseling she could look at her situation without self-pity. Her concern for Bob and the children motivated her to participate actively in making the marriage better. But her efforts brought Bob's resistance. Bob didn't want a good marriage, just the convenience of living in the same house.

Bob and Pat had opportunity for truth-seeking as they evaluated the problems in their relationship, but the opportunity went unused because Bob couldn't see beyond himself. He was trapped in a battle of impulses. One day he was overcome with guilt about his immorality. The next, he insisted he could never again love Pat. Self-focused love prohibits exploration of greater truths.

Clandestine companions. Love without responsibility has caught on. Maybe it's always been popular, but now we can watch it every evening on prime-time television. Marriage is complicated, but affairs are fun seems to be the message of many television dramas. Real life tells a different story. Extramarital affairs weave a tangled web of deception and impulse leading to personal and marital defeat. Adultery is a quick road to unhappiness.

It usually starts as an attraction. Since most spouses don't discuss extramarital attractions, this new relationship sprouts in the hidden half, protected from everyone else. The attraction causes feelings of guilt and self-condemnation, but it grows into a battle of impulses. Dark-side impulses insist these feelings can't be suppressed and glossy-side impulses insist it is immoral to experience such urges. Both impulses focus on self. Fertile secrecy and impulsive motives give way to growing intimacy and a secret relationship begins.

The process is different if duality is managed and not ignored. The initial stages of attraction are discussed with a nonreactive listener, such as a counselor, an understanding spouse, or a friend. As the feelings are explored, potential areas for growth are discovered. The truth-seeking behavior is pursued and the self-seeking behavior is lessened. Feelings of conflict are experienced within the context of openness and congruence rather than secrecy and defensiveness. Handled correctly, extramarital attractions become productive (although painful), leading to greater understanding, deeper marital love, and personal growth.

Getting type. A cartoon has two girls conversing as two boys approach. The older girl says, "Let them carry your books, but hold on to your lunch." Alfred Adler believed most individuals are the "getting type," emphasizing receiving instead of giving, even in relationships. They seek immediate gratification and quickly abandon relationships when they are no longer satisfying.

One man contemplating divorce kept telling me his wife was "a good woman." When asked to explain he said, "She's a good cook, she does laundry better than anyone I know, and she takes good care of me." If I love Lisa because she is a good cook and because she takes good care of the children, I am being impulsive, focusing on my needs. If I love Lisa because of who she is, her essence, her being, then I transcend a selfish consideration of my needs and begin to see the love as God ordained it.

In *Through the Years* Kenny Rogers sings, "I've learned what life's about by loving you through the years." Escaping a relationship because it is no longer rewarding precludes the growth resulting from long-term commitment.

It's analogous to Christian life. What happens when Christians face rough times? Some abandon the faith and move on to an easier lifestyle. They are no longer "getting" from Christianity. Others value the trials and grow as they confront new challenges. Steadfastness is growth producing. A church elder once reminded me, "Don't just do something, stand there!"

Long-term love is similar. Escaping because times are rough is impulsive and prevents growth. Working through the trials, seeking truth in a troubled relationship, causes growth and wisdom and understanding. Deep love transcends "getting."

Formula love. Answerism is convenient because it provides the answers for life's mysteries. Love is an example. Answerists encourage us to follow one of their recipes when there are problems with love. "If you're having problems in a relationship, the obvious answer is to start doing loving things and the feelings will follow." That's a recipe. Another recipe is the love-submission cycle. "If husbands are not acting loving, wives need to submit more." "If wives are not being submissive, husbands need to love more." These ideas may not be all wrong, but they are recipes resulting from answerism. Sometimes the recipes will work well, other times they won't. Such formulas often cause rebellion and greater marital dissatisfaction. And those not profiting from the advice are sometimes considered unspiritual.

The essence of love is much broader than any formula or recipe. Love cannot be reduced to easy answers. When God authored love he inbred many mysteries that defy reduction or explanation. Truth-centered love extends beyond simple answers and looks for deeper understanding.

Transcendent Love

John and Arlene's love transcends impulse. They love life and explore it together. Even after weathering parenting and grandparenting, they have a vital love, deepening with trials and victories and years. They have more trials than most, but they can handle more than most. Difficult times cause them to grow.

Transcendent love can't be explained on paper. It can only be seen in others and experienced by congruent individuals. It prospers in the midst of struggles and asks big questions without settling for easy answers. Transcendent love explores the nooks and crannies of life without secrecy or an overemphasis on "getting."

Predicting the future. The future is always uncertain. We don't know what next year will hold. Several years ago a college professor in his early thirties went home after work, lay down on the couch, had a heart attack, and died, leaving behind his wife and an eight-month-old daughter. What a tragedy! It could happen to any of us any day. The future is uncertain.

Transcendent love prospers in the midst of uncertainty. The future is not ignored, but neither is it feared. Relationships preoccupied with "what if" questions are limited to present worries. Love demands courage in spite of uncertainty. Marshall Hodge, in *Your Fear of Love*, wrote:

> If we postponed the experience and expression of love until we no longer feared it, we would postpone it

forever. Some people do appear to use their fear of love as a perpetual excuse for stalemated living—loving and trembling seem to go together. If we desire love we must learn to love in spite of our fears.

Couples anticipating marriage are often concerned about knowing the future of the relationship. Thinking about compatibility is wise, but the future remains unpredictable. A high-school friend married a Christian man after dating him several years. Five years later she was alone after her husband left with another woman. It was an unpredictable tragedy.

A professor of mine once suggested an inkblot test be given to any prospective spouse. Anticipating the future of the relationship is wise, but the most careful scrutiny cannot guarantee success. Change is difficult to predict.

Even in the midst of failure, transcendent love sees hope. Impulsive, failed relationships seem futile because they cause pain and waste valuable years. But even failed relationships produce growth. Congruent individuals leave failed relationships with greater personal wisdom. I agree with Tennyson, "'Tis better to have loved and lost than never to have loved at all."

Transcendent love is not stifled by the unpredictability of the future. It is willing to be vulnerable.

Vulnerability. Being in love is being vulnerable. Transcendent love promotes vulnerability. Abraham Maslow found that congruent people are less defensive and more vulnerable in their love relationships. Maslow summarized, "They can feel psychologically naked and still feel loved and wanted and secure."

Congruence is necessary for vulnerability. Incongruent people have difficulty believing they are lovable. They feel like imposters, trying to earn love by *doing* or by hiding their dark sides. They are less vulnerable and their love is impulsive, fixated on self-worth and personal performance.

This is a difficult concept for Christians. We often feel we need to earn Christ's love. Our efforts of *doing* fall miserably short of God's desire. He wants us to be vulnerable, sharing ourselves openly, recognizing who we are in relation to him. Remember David's powerful conclusion while confessing his adulterous relationship with Bathsheba.

> Deliver me from bloodguiltiness, O God,
> Thou God of my salvation;
> Then my tongue will joyfully sing
>   of Thy righteousness.
> O Lord, open my lips,
> That my mouth may declare Thy praise.
> For Thou dost not delight in sacrifice,
> Otherwise I would give it;
> Thou art not pleased with burnt offering.
> The sacrifices of God are a broken spirit;
> A broken and contrite heart, O God,
> Thou wilt not despise (Ps. 51:14–17).

As David was in his love for God, people with transcendent love are vulnerable because they are loved for their *being* and not their *doing*. They admit fault without defensiveness.

By emphasizing *doing*, we sometimes assume deep love involves constant togetherness. Being vulnerable in marriage allows the separateness of two lives. Both partners may have careers and separate interests. In *The Prophet*, Kahlil Gibran writes:

> And stand together yet not too near together:
> For the pillars of the temple stand apart, . . .[1]

Transcendent love prospers despite separate interests and careers.

Questions of Commitment. Traditionally, Christians have viewed marital commitment as permanent: "'till death do us part." It is difficult to maintain this Christian distinctive in the midst of compromised views of commitment.

All around us we hear that lifelong marital commitment is not possible. Tolstoy wrote, "To say that you can love one person all your life is just like saying that one candle will continue burning as long as you live." Albert Ellis has suggested that extramarital affairs may be useful for personal adjustment. In the midst of these anticommitment values, Christians have difficulty maintaining the distinctive of lifelong marital relationships.

Critics of Christianity view lifelong commitment as mindless. One psychologist commented at a workshop, "Christians don't even believe in divorce." Other participants laughed loudly as they contemplated the ridiculous views of Christians. My colleagues sometimes overlook the value of Christian commitment to fidelity and permanence in marriage.

1. Gibran, Kahlil. (1960). *The prophet.* New York: Knopf, 16.

A strong argument for permanent marriage is the lack of alternatives. Consider some of the alternatives that have been suggested. Cohabitation is widely practiced before marriage. We recently received a promotional offer from a weekly news magazine. The outside of the envelope read: "LET'S LIVE TOGETHER FOR A MONTH...*No Obligation, No commitment.*" It's a common message, but divorcing love from commitment has not been as successful as its proponents would like. Despite arguments that cohabitation better prepares couples for marriage, at least two studies have shown that cohabitants are no happier in their marriages than couples not living together prior to marriage.[2, 3]

In open marriages, first suggested by George and Nena O'Neill, partners are free to be sexually involved outside the relationship. Even the O'Neills have since noted that open marriage is very difficult for most couples since jealousy and discomfort are common.

In 1971 Alvin Toffler predicted serial marriage. I think of Sandy Duncan standing in the middle of a wheatfield advertising Wheat Thins crackers, eating "one after the other." Serial marriage is having partners, one after the other. It's the marriage-divorce-marriage-divorce cycle—the Hollywood model. On the tombstone of one actress is the inscription: *At last she sleeps alone.*

2. Hanna, S.L., and Knaub, P.K. (1981). Cohabitation before marriage: Its relationship to family strengths. *Alternative Lifestyles, 4,* 507–522.

3. Risman, B.J., Hill, C.T., Rubin Z., and Peplan, L.A. (1981) Living together in college: Implications for courtship. *Journal of Marriage and the Family, 43,* 77–83.

Alternatives to marital commitment have not worked well. I am fond of Shakespeare's words:

> Let me not to the marriage of true minds
> Admit impediments. Love is not love
> Which alters when it alteration finds,
> Or bends with the remover to remove:
> O, no! it is an ever-fixed mark,
> That looks on tempests and is never shaken;
> It is the star to every wandering bark,
> Whose worth's unknown, although his height be
>   taken
> Love's not Time's fool, though rosy lips and
>   cheeks
> Within his bending sickle's compass come;
> Love alters not with his brief hours and weeks,
> But bears it out even to the edge of doom.
> If this be error, and upon me prov'd,
> I never writ, nor no man ever lov'd.
>
> *Sonnet* 116

Divorce is often an escape preventing growth, but transcendent love grows in the midst of trials. Commitment in marriage causes opportunity for insight and understanding not otherwise possible.

Tom and Karen came for counseling after Karen's brief affair. Many might have divorced immediately, but Tom and Karen were committed to their relationship. Within a few months, they had worked through many critical issues, leaving counseling with a deeper, richer relationship than ever before. Divorce would have prevented the growth made possible by their transcendent love.

The Greatest Love

Only God, the author of love, can understand it fully. His love is pure. Just as Plato believed all worldly matter and ideas are imperfect representations of pure forms that exist elsewhere, God's love is pure and completely transcends all earthly forms. All human love is an imperfect copy of God's pure love.

How do we better understand love? By better understanding God and his character. By striving to love in ways that transcend selfish, impulsive motives we develop greater appreciation for God's love and greater ability to understand truth in his way.

> ...and that you, being rooted and grounded in love, may be able to comprehend with all the saints what is the breadth and length and height and depth, and to know the love of Christ which surpasses knowledge, that you may be filled up to all the fulness of God (Eph. 3:17b–19).

12

Seeking Truth in Pain

> It certainly cannot be without significance
> that language has created
> the concept of inward,
> of psychic, pain...
>
> Sigmund Freud
> *The Problem of Anxiety*

I love to complain. To aid me in complaining, I have several witty sayings. Murphy's Law is an example: anything that can go wrong, will go wrong. Here are some others:

The shortest distance between any two points is under construction.

A bird in hand is safer than one overhead.

Paper is always strongest at the perforations.

The probability of someone watching you is proportional to the stupidity of your action.

There are two kinds of dirt: the dark kind, attracted to light objects and the light kind, attracted to dark objects.

When I complain, I compare myself with those more fortunate. After insisting "life should be fair," I judge fairness to be painlessness. In more lucid moments I realize that things could be worse than being dealt a bad bridge hand, being stuck on a crowded freeway, or having to work a few more hours than I wanted to. By comparing myself to the homeless living under the bridges in Portland, my problems seem small. Fairness takes on new meaning.

Just as love leads to potential growth and understanding, so does pain. Unfortunately, we often view pain only as an obstacle. When we do, we become consumed in impulse and sink into greater duality. Consider the following example.

Rose, a thirty-five-year-old housewife, was disenchanted with her marriage. Her husband, Will, paid little attention to her and drank too much. After several years of marital pain, Rose came for counseling, a bundle of impulse. Dark-side impulses told Rose to avoid the pain, escape the marriage, or even to kill Will. Glossy-side impulses told her to nag Will until he gave up drinking. Of course her nagging only made Will more distant. In counseling I tried to help her consider her options from rational perspectives, but she would have nothing to do with rationality. Her efforts were directed at complaining.

Being a young intern without a lot of experience, I thought listening to Rose was the best thing I could do. So I listened intently as she complained about Will. Every time I tried to be rational, Rose started complaining. So I kept listening. After the first session she told me I was the best counselor she had seen, after seeing several others about her problem. I later realized I was not the best, just the least experienced. For several sessions I listened to Rose complain. Realizing what was happening, I finally confronted Rose about our lack of progress. When I tried to move her beyond complaining, she stopped coming and probably sought another green counselor.

Rose's situation was unfortunate, but her impulsive coping style was useless. Asking deep questions about her pain could have been useful, but she seemed unwilling. "What can I learn from this pain?" "Is this situation as bad as it seems?" "Why does God allow pain?" As with other existential issues, these questions are difficult and perhaps defy human answers, but contemplating causes growth.

Impulse and Pain

Pain viewed impulsively generates duality. Consider several possible impulsive strategies for dealing with pain.

First, *some view pain as unbearable*. From a rational framework, emotional pain is unfortunate, but rarely unbearable. For example, one client informed me that her traffic ticket was awful and terrible. Imagine for a moment the worst thing that could happen to you. For some it might be death, for others it might be total paralysis, or losing a child. Assign that "worst possible" event a "10." Now think of something half that bad and assign it a 5. Maybe losing your job or wrecking your car beyond recognition would be a 5. On our scale of 0–10, how bad is a traffic ticket? Maybe a 1 or a 2? It isn't unbearable even though it seems to be. When problems are viewed as unbearable, life strategies become reactive. Life is no longer planned in advance, but uncontrollable events begin to control one's destiny. Meism is justified by the "unbearable" nature of the pain.

Second, *emotional pain might be viewed as sinful from an impulsive perspective.* Many depressed Christians feel guilty because they have been told depression is sin. They are hesitant to get help for depression, assuming they will be accused of being unspiritual. Dave Hunt, in his book *Beyond Seduction,* asserts that all psychological problems are either problems with brain functioning or else spiritual problems. Jay Adams makes similar claims in his books. These claims may seem sensible to those without psychological problems, but they are naive and harmful to those who need psychological help. Hiding Hyde becomes common for those viewing all psychological problems as spiritual problems. They disguise their emotional pain to be accepted among Christian friends. But beneath the surface the pain is still there and growing stronger. Duality grows as the pain is denied.

Saying Christians don't have emotional pain reflects a limited perspective on Scripture. Some point to the "happiness" passages, demonstrating that we are to rejoice in the Lord and put our mind on things above. But other passages show emotional pain just as clearly. Jesus experienced emotional pain in the Garden of Gethsemane before his arrest. Many of David's psalms show tremendous emotional pain. Emotional pain in the Bible is coupled with faith, allowing a rational understanding of pain. Finding meaning in pain causes growth. Denying pain causes duality.

Third, *impulsive coping with pain sometimes leads to its advertisement.* While going through a painful bout of depression, Ken stands up in front of the church congregation during a prayer meeting and talks for forty-five minutes about his suicidal thoughts. Is he sharing because of the spiritual significance or is he soliciting sympathy? Freud wrote about the "suffering hero" fantasy where we desire others to know how much pain we are experiencing. If they really knew, we reason, they would be impressed by our strength. This glossy-side strategy is designed to elicit support from others. Getting help from others in times of emotional pain is appropriate, depending on motives. Honest cries for help do not need to be disguised in spiritual jargon.

Truth in Pain

When considered rationally, pain is valuable. Although it is never fun, it can be profitable. Pain helps us understand truth. Pain is not good, but pain can cause good.

Pain is not good. Zeno of Citum was the original stoic. Since Zeno believed a divine plan ruled the world, he contended the ultimate good was to accept all of life as part of the plan. Pain, as well as joy, was good because it was part of the plan. Indifferently accepting his fate was Zeno's goal.

Stoic philosophy became prominent in the Roman Empire until the empire began to fail. Once government corruption, crop failure, and barbarian invasions became a way of life, a new definition of "the good life" left stoicism behind. Stoicism was acceptable until pain became common.

The Stoics went too far. In viewing pain as part of the ultimate plan, they denied the negative parts of pain. Once pain became a way of life, those negative aspects could no longer be denied, and the Stoic philosophy was abandoned.

Pain is not good. It hurts! Each year in my hometown we have a show at the swimming pool. During one part of the show, teenagers put on a clown act, doing crazy stunts in the water. I love to watch them on the diving board. One guy usually rides his bike off into the water, another jumps, lands his buttocks on the diving board and belly flops into the water. It's the best part of the show. Since I'm a teenager at heart, I decided to try a fancy dive last time I went swimming. I didn't have a bicycle, so I tried the other dive. It didn't look difficult. The first time it worked all right. I walked to the edge of the board, jumped slightly, landed my seat on the diving board and bounced into the water. It was fun, but I wanted to do better. The next time, I ran to the end of the diving board to gain momentum, jumped high in the air, and tried to land my seat on the edge of the board again. Momentum causes certain problems, however, and I missed the edge of the board with my seat. Instead, I grated my back on the edge of the diving board and flopped painfully into the stinging water. That experience caused physical pain rather than emotional pain, but it sure reminded me that pain hurts. I suppose Zeno would have wanted me to meditate on the divine plan for my life as I crept painfully from the pool.

Emotional pain is often more difficult than physical pain. When a child or a spouse dies, *pain is often so overwhelming that any joy in life is overshadowed for weeks or months.* A touching Scripture passage is John 20: 10, 11. "So the disciples went away again to their own homes. But Mary was standing outside the tomb weeping. . . ." Can you imagine her despair? Jesus, the Messiah, the one who had helped her so much, was dead. Her hopes lay shattered beside his body. Her pain was great.

We grieve in response to some pain. Grief is a normal reaction to loss and is not anti-Christian. Going to heaven does not remove the need for loved ones to grieve. Those denied the opportunity to grieve usually adjust more poorly to the loss.

Bonnie's closest friend referred her for counseling. Since having a brief affair ten months earlier, her behavior had been unpredictable and her depression was not improving. As we talked, it became apparent that Bonnie still loved the man with whom she had the affair. Because her actions were sinful, her friend told her she didn't ever love this man, she only lusted after him. Shackles of guilt accompanied any grieving Bonnie did. I encouraged her to grieve. In fact, I assigned her a five-minute-daily-grief period when she was to think only about the lost relationship. Her depression improved, and she could not fill up the five-minute periods with grief. Bonnie had sinned, but she still needed to grieve. Pain hurts. To deny pain causes greater emotional turmoil and increased impulsiveness.

Another reason emotional pain is not good is that *it contributes to physical problems.* One study of 45,000 widowers in Britain showed 40 percent more deaths than expected during the six months after the death of their spouses. Death is a definite physical problem, and emotional pain appears to have some effect on death. Other studies have linked emotional pain with influenza and cancer.

Third, *pain obscures hope,* just as trees obscure the green when I go golfing. I used to say that they should put trees in the middle of the fairway where they won't get in anyone's way. Instead they put them in the rough where we all play. But later I found a hole at a nearby course with trees in the middle of the fairway. Predictably, I hit nice straight drives on that hole (I told you I love to complain). With the trees in my way, I have a hard time knowing where to hit the ball because I can't see the green. Similarly, it's hard to see hope in the midst of pain.

Pain can cause good.   Although pain is not good, it can cause good. Psychologist Lawrence Al Siebert, who has studied those surviving great emotional and physical pain, concluded in a newspaper interview:

> A typical expression of a person with a survival personality is, "I would never willingly go through anything like that again, but it was probably the best thing that could ever have happened to me."

The survivor sees value in suffering. Why would anyone see pain as good? For several reasons.

First, *pain causes a search for hope.* Paul expressed great hope writing to the Philippians. Consider some of his words of hope.

> For me to live is Christ, and to die is gain (Phil. 1:21).
> For I am confident of this very thing, that He who began

a good work in you will perfect it until the day of Christ Jesus (1:6).

Be anxious for nothing, but in everything by prayer and supplication with thanksgiving let your requests be made known to God. And the peace of God, which surpasses all comprehension, shall guard your hearts and your minds in Christ Jesus (4:6, 7).

Hope pervaded his words despite his pain at the time. His imprisonment and uncertainties about execution were overshadowed by tremendous hope. Pain stimulates the search for hope. Perhaps when we don't have enough hope it's because life is too easy.

Second, *pain broadens our world view.* In facing pain, we learn more about the nature of life. In the opening paragraph of *The Road Less Traveled,* M. Scott Peck writes that life is difficult and, paradoxically, once we learn to accept life as difficult, it is no longer difficult. Accepting pain changes our world view and life no longer seems as painful.

The beatitudes in Luke 6 and Matthew 5 remind us that pain does not go unrewarded. Blessed are the poor. Blessed are the hungry. Blessed are the persecuted. These trials create benefits. Pain broadens our world view.

Consider Peter. Before the death of Christ, Peter was impulsive. He had a foot-shaped mouth. But after the resurrection, he was a pillar in the church, zealously serving God. Three days of intense despair changed Peter's priorities forever.

On a cold January night, when our second child was three years old, we heard a loud thump in her bedroom. Lisa and I immediately responded, suspecting Sarah had fallen from the top bunk. Our first sight of Sarah has been forever etched on our memories as we saw her nightgown being quickly saturated with blood that poured from a gaping wound in her head. Two hours and nineteen stitches later, we sat talking with Sarah about the balloon she received at the hospital. Those intervening two hours had been full of emotions for Lisa and me. But they had been effective emotions, causing us to recognize Sarah's needs more accurately. Our middle child, Sarah was easily ignored with the accomplishments of our oldest and the needs of our youngest. In the wake of the accident Sarah received more parental attention than she had for months. A smile stretched across her face as she told us repeatedly of her bravery during her visit to the emergency room. That night helped Sarah realize how special she was.

Sarah's personality seemed to change after the sky-dive from the bunk bed. She became less demanding, more engaging, and happier. Lisa and I responded to Sarah differently, appreciating her more. God has used the experience for our growth. Our world view is broader as a result of that painful experience.

Third, *pain often causes growth*. Alan Watts, in an essay opposing traditional religion, suggested that ordinary religion views pain as negative, concluding that a greater spirituality can be attained by viewing pain positively as a mechanism for growth. Watts has a good point. We sometimes imply Christians will be happy and comfortable by following Christ. A church I passed several years ago had a sign advertising their air-conditioned auditorium. Our critics might be right in suggesting Christianity is too comfortably middle-class!

Scriptural accounts of suffering abound. Leaders in the early church rejoiced when they suffered. Persecution only made their commitment stronger—they grew in the midst of pain. Air-conditioned auditoriums seem less important in the light of our scriptural heritage.

Transcendence in Suffering

Mark Twain said, "Drag your thoughts away from your troubles—by the ears, by the heels, or any other way you can manage it. It's the healthiest thing a body can do." Twain's advice is compelling, but it's not satisfactory in dealing with pain.

I frequently hear clients say they have dealt with their problems by electing not to think about them. Setting an unresolved problem on a mental shelf to collect dust is rarely helpful. When the problem is confronted again, it has become infected and more complicated. Obsessing about problems is not useful, but careful exploration of pain leads to growth and greater understanding.

This paradox is similar to others suggested in this book. If we attempt to escape pain, it will consume and destroy us. If we accept pain, it can be transcended. Pain is fuel used to generate destructive explosions or power deep voyages into the unknown. One use of pain destroys and the other causes growth.

It all sounds so vague! The idea of valuing pain is difficult to convert into action and is equally difficult to transform to writing. Growing through pain is an existential issue that has to be experienced to be understood. In searching for this experience, try asking yourself some questions next time you are in pain.

What can I learn from this pain?

How does this help me understand life more broadly?

How does this help me know God?

Why do I feel the pain? What is the purpose?

What meaning can I find in this pain?

As the purpose of pain comes into focus, growth results. "Therefore I am well content with weaknesses, with insults, with distresses, with persecutions, with difficulties, for Christ's sake; for when I am weak, then I am strong" (2 Cor. 12:10).

13

Seeking Truth in Hope

In all things it is better to hope than to despair.

Goethe

Marie was dying. Her fifteen-year-old body had been invaded by a malignant brain tumor two years before. In recent months she had spent most of her time in the hospital, subjecting herself to experimental treatment procedures because they were her last chance. By the time she saw me for a neuropsychological evaluation, it was clear she was going to die.

It was a difficult evaluation. As Marie and I went through the testing procedures, a sense of despair overcame me. This young girl was to die without knowing life. She would never be engaged. She would never drive a car. She would never have a child or a job or a pension. Her few years as a teenager had been overshadowed by the devastation of cancer. It all seemed so unfair.

Marie didn't seem to share my sense of despair. Of course she didn't want to die, and tears came to her eyes at times, but she had accepted her inevitable death. She didn't seem consumed with the injustice of it all, but faced death as she had faced the past two years: with courage. Marie died within the next year, but I suspect she died with determination on her face and hope in her heart.

Ironically Marie didn't display despair before she died and yet we often despair about the most trivial disappointments. The car breaks down, or the refrigerator stops working, and we are filled with feelings of despair. We think Murphy was right. Why is our despair often covered with such a thin layer of hope while Marie's hope went to the very root of her being?

Marie wasn't any different than the rest of us. Most of us, in Marie's situation, would find a source of hope. But it's a different kind of hope. *Immediate hope* is based on impulsive motives and *transcendent hope* is truth-centered. We seek immediate hope when our refrigerator stops, but Marie reached deeper and found a hope transcending answers or solutions.

Immediate Hope

Immediate hope focuses on self. Based on impulsive motives, it looks for escape from despair. Because of its self-centered emphasis, immediate hope maintains duality.

Mr. X is having marital problems. His wife is aloof and withdrawn, their sex life is nonexistent, and they communicate poorly. Mr. X is experiencing emotional pain because of the marital breakdown. If Mr. X has immediate hope, he will look for a way to relieve the emotional pain and seek relief. Mr. X might seek a secret relationship outside the marriage. He might become intensely angry and lash out at his wife. He might use the children as pawns, trying to punish his wife through manipulation. He might resort to answerism, telling his wife she *must* start behaving in a biblical way. In any case, immediate hope may lead to greater conflict and self-defeating patterns.

Mr. Y is having similar marital problems, but has exhausted his supply of immediate hope. In the midst of his despair, he begins to recognize greater hope. Mr. Y uses his emotional pain to greater understand God's grace. He reads Hosea, recognizing that God suffers when Christians are aloof, just as he suffers when his wife is aloof. As he looks beyond himself, he experiences a deep hope—a truth-oriented hope seeing pain as a catalyst for growth.

Both Mr. X and Mr. Y have despair. But only Mr. Y has growth-producing hope. Mr. X's hope depends on resolution of the marriage. Mr. Y will have hope even if the marriage fails. The immediate hope shown by Mr. X has several distinguishing characteristics.

Solution-oriented. Mr. X needs a solution. If the problem in the marriage is not resolved, he has no hope for the future. Immediate hope seeks immediate solution.

Of course, solution seeking is useful and good. If Mr. X is able to find a solution for the marital problems, he will feel better and the marriage will be more productive. But what if Mr. X cannot find a solution? Then immediate hope fails.

Sometimes we assume everything has a solution. If Mr. X can't find the solution, he might seek the help of a marriage counselor who will "surely have the answers." But counseling isn't a fix-all. Sometimes counseling is very effective, sometimes it is ineffective, and sometimes it makes people worse! Fortunately, most people improve and few get worse. But we don't have solutions for every person or every problem.

Remember Paul's "thorn in the flesh"? He asked God to remove it three times (2 Cor. 12:8), but God saw fit to leave it with Paul. Fortunately, Paul did not limit his hope to immediate solution. His hope was deeper, transcending the immediate and looking for greater aspects of truth.

Frustration-producing. It seems strange that hope can produce frustration, but immediate hope often does. Frustration is defined as the blocking of a goal. Since immediate hope results in personal goals, when those goals are not met, frustration results. This is especially true when the personal goals, like Mr. *X*'s marriage, are outside the realm of one's control.

Traffic is a good example. For many, traffic delays are an inevitable part of life, often causing great frustration. Because we *hope* to get somewhere, we are frustrated when our progress is blocked.

Traffic used to be my nemesis. Mr. Hyde emerged whenever a slow poke in a '64 Ford pulled out in front of me going 25 miles per hour in a 45 speed zone. One day my frustrations changed because of a school assignment. In a graduate school class on psychotherapy, we were instructed to modify one of our behaviors during the course. I chose to modify my anger reaction in traffic. For several months, I spent the entire time in the car singing praise choruses. During those months, I didn't get as angry with other drivers. My habits have since changed, and I rarely become angry while driving.

Why did singing help me with my anger? Because singing helped me transcend concern for myself. Getting to my destination on time was sometimes beyond my control and was a self-centered goal—my immediate hope. Singing praises helped me look beyond myself and focus on the greater truths of God's love. As I moved beyond immediate hope, frustration lost its emotional grip. Although I no longer spend my driving time singing, I often use the time to think "big thoughts." It is my time to contemplate questions of life and meaning and move beyond myself.

Mr. *X* will be frustrated if his efforts of marital restoration are not successful. But hope goes beyond the success or failure of his marriage. As he is able to see greater hope, his frustration will become more manageable. Many people survive marital crises and grow in the process.

Self-centered. Me-centered spirituality is common. Subtle messages tell us happiness or financial prosperity come with spiritual commitment— changing Christianity into a self-serving form of religion. Occasionally people say they tried Christianity, but it didn't work for them. That's not the point. If Christianity is true, then whether it "works for me" or not is irrelevant.

Immediate hope reinforces me-centered spirituality. "If you need a new car, just pray for it, and God will provide." "If you need a better marriage, just seek Christian counseling, and it will get better." "If you need more business, give your efforts up to God and he will send more business your way." These "name-it-and-claim-it" messages are based on immediate hope and focused on self. *Do we believe in the power of Jesus Christ because of what he can do for us?*

God-centered spirituality recognizes that truth extends far beyond self. I pray for sunshine for a picnic, and the farmer next door prays for rain so his corn will grow. God considers more than my needs. Immediate hope leads to despair when the rain spoils the picnic. Truth-centered hope leads to disappointment, but disappointment tempered with an awareness that God has a "bigger picture."

Transcendent Hope

Transcendent hope focuses on truth. Remember Marie? Remember Mr. Y? Both were able to look beyond immediate resolution. They were able to look beyond self-centered needs and find peace in the midst of turmoil.

Coping with despair. Whereas immediate hope looks for an end to difficulties, transcendent hope looks for meaning in the midst of despair. Figure 13 shows four options for coping with despair. The first three work well in some situations, but not with irresolvable or long-standing pain.

The first option is *to avoid despair*. Immediate hope seeks solutions. It is reasonable and good to avoid despair when possible, but sometimes despair is unavoidable. When Marie first learned of her brain tumor, she and her parents tried to avoid the despair through medical treatment. They tried many medical interventions without success. They could not avoid the cancer, and Marie died despite their efforts.

It's like an end sweep in football. To avoid defenders, halfbacks run to the edge of the field and then attempt

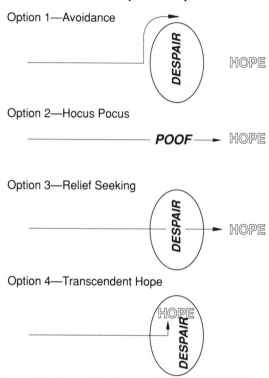

Figure 13 Four alternative ways to find hope in despair.

Option 1—Avoidance

DESPAIR   HOPE

Option 2—Hocus Pocus

POOF → HOPE

Option 3—Relief Seeking

DESPAIR → HOPE

Option 4—Transcendent Hope

HOPE
DESPAIR

to turn upfield. Sometimes they successfully avoid the defense and are able to gain many yards on the play. Other times, they run toward the sidelines, but the defense runs with them, and they are tackled without gain. Similarly, sometimes our efforts to avoid despair are successful and other times we are not able to elude our unpleasant circumstances.

The second option is *to deny despair in order to feel hope*. Denial is a useful psychological defense, but eventually it obscures truth and causes problems. Christian platitudes are sometimes efforts to deny despair. By spiritual "hocus pocus" we sometimes think we can remove pain.

One Christian described a traumatic incident after his eighteen-year-old son died in a drowning accident. As he left the funeral home where he was making preparations for the memorial service, a well-meaning Christian walked up and asked if he was the one who just lost his son. When the grieving father answered affirmatively, the other man smiled, patted him on the shoulder and said, "Praise the Lord!"

Christianity doesn't require us to deny despair. Saying "Praise the Lord!" to someone who has just lost his son is a platitude, ineffectively designed to remove despair. Despair is not so easily removed.

The third option is *to see hope as relief, the TGIF mentality*. In seeking relief in his marriage, Mr. X sees hope only as the absence of marital conflict. This relief-seeking hope causes football players to count the days until "daily doubles" are over, or college students to number the days of class left before summer break. It is the hope I begin to have on the ninth hole of the golf course, recognizing my misery will soon be over. But relief doesn't always come in life. Sometimes, like Paul's thorn, pain continues relentlessly. Seeking relief is fine, but not always effective.

Transcendent hope is the fourth option. Transcendent hope flourishes in the midst of despair. For example, Mr. Y does not have hope only if his marriage gets better (option 3), but has hope even in the midst of marital conflict. His hope goes beyond personal comfort and is founded deeply in God's truth.

This is not asceticism. Mr. Y is not seeking out despair because he thinks suffering will make him more spiritual. Indeed he avoids despair whenever possible, but in the midst of inescapable despair he is able to see hope.

Transcendent hope characterized Paul's letter to the Philippians. Paul found hope in God's truth despite his unfortunate circumstances. Never did Paul hinge his hope on his release from prison. His hope transcended self and embraced God's greater truths.

I try to distinguish between immediate and transcendent hope in counseling. Often clients do not learn to cope with a trial until they are able to see value in the trial. Once they see value and truth, they are able to transcend self-centeredness and experience true hope.

Beyond myopia.   Missionary Bert Elliott notes that we can't see the sun if we have silver dollars placed over our eyes. The sun is big and cosmic. The dollar is small and can add to self-centeredness. We cannot see the bigness of God's truth with dollars over our eyes.

Those seeing the big picture are often the ones who have had the dollars stripped away from their eyes. Marie had no immediate hope. She was going to die. Her dollar had been stripped away, and she was forced to look for a greater hope. Paul had no immediate hope. He was imprisoned with a possible death sentence. His dollar had been stripped away and in transcendent hope he wrote to the Philippians.

Elisabeth Kübler-Ross studied the process of dying and concluded we go through emotional stages in confronting death. Although recent evidence casts doubt on the validity of her stage theory, it is instructive to remember that her final stage of adjustment—not reached by all—is *acceptance. Denial, anger, bargaining,* and *depression* are gone, and a restful acceptance of death results. All possibilities of hope have been removed, and it somehow seems okay.

Maybe we don't experience transcendent hope because we have too many sources of immediate hope. When immediate hope is stripped away, we see the big picture more clearly.

Why are Christians in religiously oppressed countries reported to be so zealous? Could it be because they don't have the dollars in their eyes? They worship in fear of death, but choose to worship because they seek truth above self. In free countries it is easy to worship for other reasons. We sometimes forget to take the dollars out of our eyes.

Hopelessness is a stimulus for seeking greater hope. In describing the faith of Abraham, Paul writes:

> In hope against hope he believed, in order that he might become a father of many nations, according to that which had been spoken, "So shall your descendents be" (Rom. 4:18).

Abraham had no immediate hope to have a child. Solutions defied reason. But Abraham had a greater hope in God's purpose, demonstrated later by his willingness to offer his only son as a sacrifice. Abraham's transcendent hope opposed immediate hope "in hope against hope."

Paul also found hope in the midst of hopelessness. After realizing his thorn would never be removed he found a greater hope in his ailment.

> For if I do wish to boast I shall not be foolish, for I shall be speaking the truth; but I refrain from this, so that no one may credit me with more than he sees in me or hears from me. And because of the surpassing greatness of the revelations, for this reason, to keep me from exalting myself, there was given me a thorn in the flesh, a messenger of Satan to buffet me—to keep me from exalting myself (2 Cor. 12:6, 7)!

Paul lost immediate hope and gained a greater hope in the midst of despair. The dollar was stripped from his eye, and he could see God's purpose.

Mixing of Hope

Both immediate hope and transcendent hope are appropriate. One without the other is problematic. Mr. X has immediate hope without transcendent hope. As a result, he is unable to see beyond his own needs and continues to look for ineffective solutions to a problem that may be beyond solution.

On the other hand, transcendent hope without immediate hope results in unnecessary pain and the risk of asceticism. If pain can be avoided without compromising morality, why not avoid it? Pain is not intrinsically good. For example, Mr. X's seeking help for marital problems is appropriate. If the pain of marital conflict can be resolved, discomfort will be prevented. Immediate hope allows us to avoid pain when possible.

By mixing hope we integrate both immediate and transcendent hope as needed. We seek relief from despair whenever possible and experience immediate hope. But when despair remains, our hope extends beyond the immediate and looks for meaning and truth. These times are often the richest and most growth producing, yet the most painful and uncomfortable.

Psychiatrist Victor Frankl, imprisoned in a concentration camp during World War II, concluded that suffering causes us to find meaning. As we find value in pain and suffering, our hope transcends the immediate, we move beyond impulses and seek truth.

14

Seeking Truth in Grace

> Lord Jesus Christ, today I want to live my life as
> an expression of your love rather than as an effort
> to earn or deserve your love. Like Paul, I have
> tried about everything to prove my worth.
> Nothing satisfies. I am weary of doing the right
> thing because of guilt and not grace. Thank you
> for the limitless power of your love which sets
> me free from a guilted cage to fly and soar to new
> heights of joyous praise today. Amen.[1]

> Lloyd John Ogilvie

On a hot August day my old Plymouth Duster
began to spew forth steam from its clogged radiator.
After pulling to the side of the road and evaluating the
situation, I realized the radiator was nearly empty. Ten
miles from the nearest city and nine hundred miles
from my college destination, a dark cloud of despair
settled over me as I planned my next action. The vast
nothingness of I–5 in central Oregon was shattered
only by an occasional vehicle speeding by.

---

1. Ogilvie, Lloyd John. (1974). Free from the guilted cage. From *Let God Love You*. Waco, Tex.: Word, Inc.

As I began to plan my hitchhike to the nearest town, a man in a pickup truck pulled off the freeway and offered assistance. Not only was he willing to help me, he had a 200 gallon drum of water in the back of his pickup! After cooling off the engine, he filled my radiator with water, allowing me to make it to the next town for repairs.

In the midst of my skepticism of human motives, the smile on that man's face stands out as a brilliant memory etched forever in my understanding of human nature. He wanted no money, no fame, no favors. He only wanted to help. Like the good Samaritan, he would take nothing in return for his free gift.

Grace demonstrates the most noble of human intentions. Ultimately all grace is modeled after the greatest grace, God's acceptance of humankind. Grace is bigger and brighter than truth found in love, pain, and hope because grace makes love unconditional, pain bearable, and hope substantive.

The road from impulsivity to rationality is paved with grace. *Doing* is emphasized less and *being* is emphasized more.

If-Then Mentality

Remember "if-then" statements from high school mathematics and college logic courses. *"If* it rains on Tuesday, *then* we will not have the baseball game." *"If* Patty does not act friendly, *then* I will know she is holding a grudge." *"If* I do not study, *then* I will not pass the test."

If-then statements are logical. It is more difficult for us to imagine *if-less thens.* "I love you regardless of what you do to me." "I will help you even if you can't pay me for my time." "I will care about you no matter how evil your life has been." These statements of grace transcend an *if-then* mentality.

Don Francisco captured the essence of God's *if-less then* toward mankind in his song, *I Don't Care Where You've Been Sleeping*.

> I loved you long before the time your eyes first saw the day
> And everything I've done has been to help you on the way;
> But you took all that you wanted then at last you took your leave,
> And traded off a Kingdom for the lies that you believed.
>
> I don't care where you've been sleeping,
> I don't care who's made your bed;
> I already gave My life to set you free;
> There's no sin you can imagine that is stronger than My love,
> And it's all yours if you'll come home again to Me.
>
> Although you've chosen darkness with its miseries and fears,
> Although you've gone so far from Me and wasted all those years,
> Even though My name's been spattered by the mire in which you lie
> I'd take you back this instant if you'd turn to Me and cry.
>
> I don't care where you've been sleeping,
> I don't care who's made your bed;
> I already gave My life to set you free;

There's no sin you can imagine that is stronger than My
 love,
And it's all yours if you'll come home again to Me.

When you come back to your senses and you see who's
 been to blame,
Remember all the good things that were yours with just
 My name;
Then don't waste another thought before you change
 the way you're bound
I'll be running out to meet you if you'll only turn
 around.

I don't care where you've been sleeping,
I don't care who's made your bed;
I already gave My life to set you free;
There's no sin you can imagine that is stronger than My
 love,
And it's all yours if you'll come home again to Me.[2]

Christian Rationality

Most agree that God's image has been given to all
humans, not just to Christians. But throughout the
New Testament, Paul refers to the "old self" and the
"new self," implying only Christians have the new self.
What can be said of the "new nature" that Paul implies
only Christians have? After presenting my model of
duality to students in a counseling class, one student
asked me this very question. I had no answer. I was not
able to tell him how Christians are different from non-
Christians in experiencing the rational life motive.
Like all professors, I was able to come up with a few

well-chosen (but meaningless) words to defend myself, but we both knew there was a gaping hole in my model.

Several weeks later I was jogging with a colleague and sharing the model with him. "You're right," he said, "we really need to understand God's grace." That was it! The reason Christians have a "new self" is that we can understand the truth of God's grace. Paul concluded the same thing in Romans 8: 1, 2 after despairing of conflict between the old and new nature.

> There is therefore now no condemnation for those who are in Christ Jesus. For the law of the Spirit of life in Christ Jesus has set you free from the law of sin and of death.

Grace and Impulse

Grace and impulse are completely incompatible. Impulse focuses on self and grace *must* transcend self because we don't deserve grace. Grace can never be understood with an *if-then* mentality. All the impulsive coping strategies—hiding Hyde, hiding Jekyll, answerism, and meism—miss the essence of grace.

Hiding Hyde.   Kara was an expert at hiding Hyde. Even after several months of therapy, she hadn't told me what really troubled her. The pain of revealing Mr. Hyde was too great and hiding seemed easier. Kara saw God's grace as sufficient, but only for others. In order for her to receive God's grace, she had to earn it.

Pointing out the double standard seemed an easy solution, but it was no solution at all. Kara knew she had a double standard. She knew it was not reasonable that God loved others regardless of their behavior, but only loved her based on her performance. She had the head knowledge, but it didn't change the inner conflict. Her efforts continued to be focused on earning God's grace. "I must do better" seemed to be her life motto. Because Kara was engaged in a battle of impulses, dark side versus glossy side, she couldn't see beyond herself and accept the greater truth of God's grace.

Hiding Jekyll. In hiding Jekyll, grace is seen as an opportunity to take advantage of others. Grace becomes a means of self-fulfillment. Most of us are hesitant to give hitchhikers a ride because of this phenomenon. We've heard stories of drivers offering rides to hitchhikers who have abducted them, stolen their cars, and so forth. To the antisocial hitchhiker, the grace of others is an opportunity for personal gain. As with hiding Hyde, self is the primary focus and the truth of grace is missed.

Answerism. With answerism, grace is cheapened. A shallow grace, focusing on personal performance, results. Evangelicals often talk of "cheap grace." We are told that when we sin, we act as if God's grace was cheap and minimize the suffering of Jesus. My understanding is different. I believe sin makes grace abound. In response to sin we see how vast God's grace really is. Our "cheap grace" theology is what cheapens grace by implying God's grace just barely covers some of our sins.

You may be thinking of Romans 6:1, 2 where Paul writes, "What shall we say then? Are we to continue in sin that grace might increase? May it never be!..." But remember Paul writes this clause only to qualify his main argument found in the previous chapter. Paul's argument is "...where sin increased, grace abounded all the more" (5:20). Sin doesn't make grace cheap, it makes grace abound. Sin brings either self-condemnation (self-focus) or a profound sense of the forgiving nature of God who loves regardless of performance (truth-focus). Grace abounds in the midst of sin. Reducing God's acceptance to our *if-then* mentality cheapens his grace.

When I sin, I'm not a victim of cheap grace, but of cheap faith. If, in faith, I really grasp the magnitude of God's grace, then my life will display faith and evidence godly works. Conversely, if my faith is not big enough to comprehend the *if-less then* of God's grace, my works will demonstrate impulsive battles and self-defeating behaviors.

Meism. Meism also misses the essence of grace. Grace is seen as nice but irrelevant to the substance of true achievement. Only things achieved through personal effort are valuable to the meist. "You get what you work for" is the message of meism. Christians easily slip into this mentality. Jim and Tammy Bakker felt robbed of their ministry. They built the ministry and wanted it back. Their emphasis on personal achievement and wealth predominate their thinking.

Grace and the Big Picture

Grace is very big—much bigger than a theological concept for Sunday-morning sermons. *More than any other truth, grace transcends self and separates our being from our doing.* Understanding grace requires the rational life motive because it cannot be understood on an impulsive level. David Seamands, in his excellent book, *Healing for Damaged Emotions*, writes:

> We read, we hear, we believe a good theology of grace. But that's not the way we live. We believe grace in our heads but not in our gut level feelings or in our relationships. There's no other word we throw around so piously.[3]

Many Christians speak of grace as if they understand it. But they live differently, investing effort in earning God's favor, condemning themselves when they fail, and focusing on how evil their hidden half is. They talk about grace, but they attempt to understand it with impulsive thinking. Glossy-side impulses escalate and self-defeating guilt results. Grace must be separated from personal performance to understand it.

Understanding grace goes beyond rationality also. As Kierkegaard noted, issues of faith extend beyond reason and can never be understood with reason alone. Some questions cannot be answered. "Why did God choose to demonstrate his grace through the sacrificial death of Christ?" "How can we know for sure God exists?" "How can we know that Christians understand more of God's truth than Moslems, Hindus, or Buddhists?" These questions go beyond human rationality, requiring a leap of faith.

Although we cannot reduce faith to a purely rational concept, it is rational in another sense. We believe because we have seen sufficient evidence. In Francis

3. Seamands, David. (1981). *Healing for damaged emotions*. Wheaton, Ill.: Victor Books, 30.

Schaeffer's terms, it is not a blind faith but a simple faith. Similarly, although we can't completely comprehend God's grace, it helps to consider the other attributes of God. His grace is consistent with his immutability, his steadfast love, and his mercy.

Worm Theology

"Amazing grace how sweet the sound, that saved a wretch like me." I love the song, but object to the second line. Perhaps I am a wretch. Perhaps I am a worm as the lyrics to another great hymn suggest. Certainly I am when comparing myself to God's glory. But why compare? Focusing on my wretchedness keeps me from focusing on God's greatness. God's grace would be just as magnificent even if I weren't a wretch!

A man came up to me after a conference meeting and told me of his fondness for the doctrine of total depravity. He argued that our current society has lost the biblical emphasis on the unworthiness of humankind. I disagreed actively, suggesting we have instead lost the equally biblical emphasis on the greatness of God's grace. Grappling with the enormity of grace forces one beyond self. We were able to disagree and still be friendly, but I found myself observing him closely for the remainder of the conference.

The following day on the volleyball court, the same man showed the reality of his belief. While the rest of us attempted to have an amusing game of co-ed volleyball, he was invested in the competition. At first, this didn't seem unusual. Almost every time I play volleyball there is at least one person who is more competitive than most, expressing disappointment over others' missed shots, poor efforts, and so forth, but this man was *different*. In addition to condemning others for playing poorly, he condemned himself. Throughout several games, he muttered about how poorly he was playing and how much better he *should* be doing. His volleyball philosophy was consistent with his worm theology.

Worm theology and meism are similar. Both focus on personal performance and both assume self-worth is based on performance. Worm theology leads to a deflated self-esteem while meism leads to inflated self-worth, but both focus on self. Self-focus, in turn, can lead to shallow spirituality. Paul wrote, "You have been severed from Christ, you who are seeking to be justified by law; you have fallen from grace" (Gal. 5:4). God doesn't want us to moan in our inadequacies, to be justified by works. He doesn't value us because of our performance. Indeed, our sins are completely removed from God's view. I think God was disappointed that my Christian brother couldn't enjoy his volleyball game, just as he is disappointed when we can't ponder his grace because we are too busy thinking of ourselves as worms.

Wonder Theology

Wonder theology is an alternative to worm theology. Brett knows the difference now. When he first came for counseling, he was overwhelmed by guilt. His sexual behavior had caused many problems, and the emotional consequences were catching up with him. During our first session he seemed compelled to confess his awfulness and grovel in his worthlessness. I listened, but didn't actively agree that he was awful. In fact, I didn't talk about his behavior at all. He already knew his behavior was wrong. Instead we started considering some bigger questions. "What does grace mean?" "How could God accept Brett as if he had never sinned?" Without looking for answers, we began to explore the profound wonder of God's grace.

Brett did better than most. He gave up his worm theology and began contemplating the wonder of God within a few weeks. His symptoms improved, his behaviors changed, and his understanding of God matured. For many, abandoning worm theology requires more time and work. But rarely do others experience as much pain as Brett. His pain opened his mind to see a bigger picture of God's grace.

In some ways I may be like a worm. When I compare myself to a Creator with such awesome power, I'm pretty small. I'm worthless. In other ways, I'm important. God put his image in me and valued me enough to send his son to be my sacrificial atonement. I'm worthwhile. But this paradox is irrelevant because it doesn't matter whether I'm worthless or worthwhile. It's more significant that God's love doesn't depend on *my* value.

Responding to Children

Grace is not only a theological concept. I talk frequently of grace with clients who don't share my Christian perspectives. Grace is a powerful psychological concept. Grace is the essence of a parent's love for a child.

Dr. D. James Kennedy has observed:

> Psychiatrists and psychologists have discovered that a
> child is not, even on the most rudimentary level, able to
> love unless he has been loved by his parents. It is a
> tragedy when some parents, because of feelings of being
> unloved, have a child so that the child will love them.
> The child desperately needs to be loved; and if the child
> is brought into the world to provide that which is
> lacking in the parent, then the vicious circle continues
> and only the love of Jesus Christ breaking in can end it.

Love that demands something in return is love without
grace. Conversely, love mingled with grace demands no
performance in return. There are many good books on
parenting, but parents who actively demonstrate grace
will have better results than parents who read every
new book but love conditionally.

Lest I present my own glossy side, let me clearly
acknowledge that I'm not a perfect parent. Come to
think of it, I'm not perfect at anything. Sometimes I'm
an average dad, relaxing in solitude while my kids play
in another room. Sometimes I'm a good dad, playing
games and having fun with my children or correcting
their conduct with gentle firmness. Sometimes I'm a
bad dad, subtly communicating with my tone of voice
that they are less worthwhile because of what they
have just done.

With Lisa's help, my children compiled some perspectives on life when they were younger. I especially
liked their account entitled "Pretending House."

Pretending House

You need two people and a baby. The baby could be a

doll, a teddy bear, or your little sister. Someone's always the Mom (whoever is a girl and pretty big). Someone's always the Dad (whoever is a boy and pretty big). If you don't have a boy the biggest girl is the Dad. Then we put the baby to bed (you have to pray with her first) and have some pretend tea, or toast, taco or peanut butter sandwiches. When the baby does something like dig in the pretend plants, you spank her. Then we talk to her and hug her. Playing pretend house is sort of like real life even.

I don't like my children to think of me as a spanker since I use it so rarely in discipline, but I like the way my children described their spankings. Spankings were followed with affirmation. My children are worthwhile to me, as yours are to you, even when they have transgressed. Expressing acceptance and love is an integral part of good discipline.

My children will see faults in me as they grow older, just as I now see faults in my parents. But in the midst of those faults, I want them to experience grace as I experienced grace in my home. There weren't demands for perfection when I brought home a report card. I wasn't humiliated because of my disobedience. My parents didn't use their love as a lever to manipulate my behavior. They weren't perfect parents, but they understood grace and showed it to me. Because of them I now better understand grace and try to show it to my children.

Our perceptions of God may be closely related to our views of our parents. A child who does not see a parent's grace may have difficulty understanding God's grace. If my children can understand their worth doesn't depend on their performance, then they can understand God's grace and avoid the self-focus of me-ism or worm theology.

Responding to Failure

We are fundamentally dual people, living in impulse and rationality—the Jekyll/Hyde syndrome. Because we are dual, we inevitably fail. Responding to failure becomes important in avoiding future battles of impulse.

Remember bulimic Brenda from chapter 4? Each time she binged, she convinced herself it would never happen again. This time she had enough strength to be perfect. Of course these thoughts were glossy-side impulses demanding perfection, eventually giving way to dark-side impulses when she binged again. As Brenda progressed in treatment, she started responding differently to failure.

First, *after treatment Brenda realized she would fail again*. Brenda binged about once every two months after treatment; a good improvement from the once-a-day pattern she had when she first sought help. We will always fail again unless we die first. Despite the urgings of the glossy side, we will never be perfect as humans.

Second, *Brenda learned that failure didn't reduce her worth*. Her value no longer depended on her performance. She learned a form of grace. In evangelicalism we often miss the separateness between value and performance. God's grace and our performance are unrelated. Grace, as Brenda learned, is unconditional.

Third, *glossy-side impulses controlled Brenda less after treatment.* She still had a "little voice" telling her to eat only celery and to exercise at least an hour each day, but she filtered those impulses with rational thoughts. Before, she wouldn't eat bread, fearful it would cause her to binge. Now she allowed herself to eat bread and other formerly "forbidden" foods. She became a whole person, in touch with her impulses and her ability to reason.

Destroying Impulses/Destroying Grace

Duality is uncomfortable, making it natural for us to think it can be escaped. But our efforts to destroy dark-side impulses result in escalation of glossy-side impulses as battles of impulses are fertilized and self-focus becomes a way of life. In the midst of the battles we can't see grace. The bigger picture becomes obscured as the *shoulds* of the glossy side battle the *wants* of the dark side.

Palliative coping strategies relieve the battle but keep the focus on self, causing missed opportunities for growth, shallow spirituality, and lack of rationality. By attempting to eliminate impulses we prevent ourselves from understanding God's grace.

> Then the Lord said,
> "Because this people draw near with their words
> And honor Me with their lip service,
> But they remove their hearts far from Me,
> And their reverence for Me consists of tradition learned
>   *by rote*,
> Therefore behold, I will once again deal marvelously
>   with this people, wondrously marvelous;

And the wisdom of their wise men shall perish,
And the discernment of their discerning men shall be
  concealed" (Isa. 29:13, 14).

God is grieved by our traditionalized spirituality.
Glossy-side impulses are ritualistic and not relational.
In response, he has dealt marvelously with us as he
promised. God gives grace to drive us away from our
traditional self-focused rituals. He wants us to worship
him in truth.

What Do We Need?

What do we need in evangelicalism today? We need
whole persons who understand grace. We certainly
don't need more newspaper scandals or more sexual
game playing. We don't need bigger ministries, more
popular television evangelists, or Christian amuse-
ment parks. We don't need more money or bigger orga-
nizations or larger budgets. We don't need more
eloquent pastors or persuasive authors or cogent
speakers. We don't need more psychologists or fewer
psychologists or more seminaries or fewer seminaries
or bigger congregations or smaller congregations or a
more supportive government or more persecution. We
simply need *sincerity*. We need Christians who understand God's grace and live obediently. We need *whole
persons*.

Grace allows wholeness. Because God accepts us and
loves us despite our hidden half, we know his grace
doesn't depend on our performance. We can be whole
before God, assured of his love. Recognizing our com-
pleteness in God allows us to rest in the deep joy of true

spirituality and consistent obedience. It allows us to focus on God, to look beyond the unworthiness of humankind, and to accept others openly.

We experience wholeness only as we abandon the battle of impulses. Engaged in a compelling search for truth, we experience love, pain, hope, and grace in ways that transcend self. God's grace begins to absorb self-interest and impulses become stepping-stones to greater understanding and wholeness.